ANALOGICAL INVESTIGATIONS

Western philosophy and science are responsible for constructing some powerful tools of investigation, aiming at discovering the truth, delivering robust explanations, verifying conjectures, showing that inferences are sound and demonstrating results conclusively. By contrast, reasoning that depends on analogies has often been viewed with suspicion. Professor Lloyd first explores the origins of those Western ideals, criticises some of their excesses and redresses the balance in favour of looser, admittedly non-demonstrative analogical reasoning. For this, he takes examples from both ancient Greek and Chinese thought and from the materials of recent ethnography to show how different ancient and modern cultures have developed different styles of reasoning. He also develops two original but controversial ideas, that of semantic stretch (to cast doubt on the literal/metaphorical dichotomy) and the multidimensionality of reality (to bypass the realism versus relativism and nature versus nurture controversies).

G. E. R. LLOYD is Emeritus Professor of Ancient Philosophy and Science at the University of Cambridge, former Master of Darwin College, Cambridge, and Senior Scholar in Residence at the Needham Research Institute, Cambridge. He is the author of twenty-two books and editor of four, and was knighted for 'services to the history of thought' in 1997.

T0384847

ANALOGICAL INVESTIGATIONS

*Historical and Cross-cultural Perspectives on
Human Reasoning*

G. E. R. LLOYD

CAMBRIDGE
UNIVERSITY PRESS

CAMBRIDGE
UNIVERSITY PRESS

University Printing House, Cambridge CB2 8BS, United Kingdom

Cambridge University Press is part of the University of Cambridge.

It furthers the University's mission by disseminating knowledge in the pursuit of education, learning and research at the highest international levels of excellence.

www.cambridge.org
Information on this title: www.cambridge.org/9781107518377

© G. E. R. Lloyd 2015

First published 2015

Printed in the United Kingdom by Clays, St Ives plc

A catalogue record for this publication is available from the British Library

ISBN 978-1-107-10784-7 Hardback
ISBN 978-1-107-51837-7 Paperback

Contents

List of diagrams   *page* vi

Introduction   1

1   On the very possibility of mutual intelligibility   10

2   The multiple valences of comparatism   29

3   Analogies, images and models in ethics: some first-order and
    second-order observations on their use and evaluation in
    ancient Greece and China   43

4   Analogies as heuristic   58

5   Ontologies revisited   88

6   Conclusions   109

Glossary of Chinese terms   122
Notes on editions   124
Bibliography   125
Index   136

Diagrams

1 Euclid, *Elements* I 5.   *page* 62
2 Alternative Proof of Euclid, I 5.   63
3 Euclid, *Elements* I 47.   64
4 Qu's reconstruction of *gou gu* diagram and of its construction.   65
5 Sam Loyd's puzzle.   66
6 Sam Loyd Junior's variation.   67
7 Kepler, *Paralipomena to Witelo*, ch. 4.   69
8 Hexagram 27 *Yi.*   76

Introduction

Western philosophy and science are jointly responsible for constructing some amazingly powerful tools of investigation, aimed at discovering the truth, delivering explanations, verifying conjectures, showing that inferences are sound and proving results conclusively.[1] We use the scientific method and logic to achieve all that, and further back those two depend not just on the precision and accuracy of measurements and the replicability of results, but also on the clarity of definition, the avoidance of ambiguity and above all the univocity of terms. If those criteria are not met, the enterprise aborts.

These ideas and practices as we know them today happen to have been developed first, in most cases, in Europe, though adumbrations of several of them are to be found elsewhere. But how should we evaluate our European legacy? Most people throughout the world, and not just Westerners, probably assume straightforwardly that those tools represent an unqualified success, for have they not been responsible for most of the progress humans have ever made, both in understanding and in improving material welfare, not least in the matter of our health and ability to combat disease?

But doubts and criticisms have also been and continue to be expressed. One group of dissenters resents the hegemonic tones in which the West

---

[1] Thus in a recent article de Jong and Betti (2010) argue that the essentials of the Aristotelian concept of science, in particular the notions of definition, axiomatics, demonstration and method as set out in the *Posterior Analytics*, have been a dominant influence from Aristotle's day to ours. They instance not just ancient authors such as Proclus, but also most of the denizens of seventeenth-century science, Descartes, Newton, Pascal, Spinoza, Leibniz, the Port Royal logicians (cf. the next note), and on to Wolff, Kant, Bolzano and even Frege. They cite Dijksterhuis (1986: 464–5) in support, and also Randall's claim (1961: 63, echoing Whitehead on Plato) that 'the whole great literature on method that fills the scientific writings of the seventeenth century is at bottom a series of footnotes to the *Organon* of Aristotle'. There are obvious exaggerations and oversimplifications in this thesis, notably because it downplays the objections to Aristotelianism that were regularly expressed by the likes of Bacon, Hume and many others. But few would deny the importance of that influence, and the puzzle then becomes to identify the reasons for its persistence, only partially to be accounted for by the way in which, from Aquinas on especially, Christian theology exploited Aristotelian ideas to bolster its claims to demonstrate the truth.

implicitly or explicitly claims superior rationality, intelligence, know-how, although that resentment does not of itself further the evaluation of the key ideas and methods. Some dismiss the claims for better understanding as a mirage, with the relativist's argument that everyone's notion of understanding is dependent on subjective or at least society-specific norms. Even claims to increase material prosperity are sometimes countered by pointing to the harm and destruction that have followed in the wake of technological advance, from weapons of mass destruction to global warming.

However, the debate to date pays less attention than it might to pressing the analysis of what I have called those tools of investigation. As a historian I am aware of some of the contingent circumstances in which certain crucial ideas were developed, often starting in ancient Greece. As a comparativist I can use other cultures to trace trajectories of intellectual development and ambition that differ from those we are used to in the West. The studies that I have gathered together in this book contain some philosophical reflections on the multiple tracks that human endeavours to achieve both understanding and the control of the environment have followed. These investigations are then 'analogical', in the broad sense in which I shall use that term, in two ways: first in the sense that they are comparative, probing the similarities and differences between what I have called those trajectories, but, secondly, in a further sense in that it turns out that the use of analogies, models, images and similarities (even though often viewed with suspicion) is all-pervasive. The object of the exercise is to test both the strengths and the weaknesses of common assumptions about what is held up as the right, indeed often the only viable, track.

There are several fundamental questions we have to tackle first, to do with language itself, with how we express our thoughts and how, and within what limits, we can understand others. We encounter obvious problems when we try to translate from one natural language to another – where we typically search for some equivalent, comparable or analogous form of words to convey what is said in another language – but we can raise problems also about the level of comprehension achievable even when all those engaged in the communicative exchange share the same natural language. The problem of reference takes us to the question of what there is to be referred to. The indeterminacy or inscrutability of reference (Quine) has often been discussed in relation, in the first instance, to individual speech acts. But it is recognised that the issue raises a fundamental problem to do with an inevitable feature of all language use, namely the use of general terms. It was all very well for Plato, in the *Phaedrus* (265e), to suggest that what he called collection and division should carve nature at the joints.

But are there such joints to carve, and what is the nature they belong to? In this instance indeed we can cross-reference to another culture that also raised the question of the relation between Names and Objects, namely ancient China, though we shall see that the focus of interest there was very different. When names are said to have to tally with objects, that is chiefly a matter of ensuring that social distinctions are maintained, an issue of social order, not just one of linguistic accuracy.

The notion that science and philosophy both, in their different ways, deal with a single determinate external reality is one of the foundational tenets of modernity. It too has its history which brings to light many competing interpretations of what that reality consists in and how access to it is to be had. To reject any such claims in the name of a radical cultural relativity seems a counsel of despair. How then can we find a way through the apparent impasse with which we are faced? Again a judicious use of history, philosophy, cognitive science, comparative studies and social anthropology can be brought to bear to suggest tentative resolutions of a sort.

Many of the leading questions implicate the notion of analogy and related ideas (similarity, models, images), whether as a movement of thought that we use to describe and explain phenomena, or as a characteristic that those phenomena are assumed to manifest. The structures of genera and species that form the subject-matter of inquiry in many disciplines presuppose ordered relations of similarity and difference, and similarity itself may be considered the genus within which analogy falls, though that may be to impose a questionable orderliness on the similarities of types of similarity itself. More basically still, the general terms that any natural language supplies imply that the species and particulars that come under them exhibit similarities that justify their being grouped together.

In my first book, *Polarity and Analogy* (Lloyd 1966), I considered those two as modes of argumentation in early Greek thought, using that term 'modes of argumentation' to cover both explicit argument schemas and overarching theories, totalising ones offering cosmological accounts as well as more specific explanations of particular phenomena. Analogies apprehend or postulate similarities or connections, often suggesting inferences and extensions of the similarities apprehended. 'Polarities' was the term I used for modes of reasoning that focus on pairs of opposites (of different kinds) and again use those oppositions as the basis of schemas of argumentation, as when two opposites are held to present mutually exclusive and exhaustive alternatives, and one proceeds from the rejection of one to the confirmation of the other. I brought to bear some comparative material from social anthropology and my limited study of other ancient societies, China included, but my chief target was ancient Greece itself. I would now say that a similar investigation, of the various manifestations of comparing and contrasting, and of the presuppositions made concerning what is there to be compared and contrasted, can and should be mounted in relation to human reasoning of every period and in every culture. I cannot of course do justice to the global problems in all their complexity. But I aim to say enough to make a start in the due evaluation of those tools of investigation that I have identified. Analogy is indispensable, but it must be combined with critical assessment, though not in the expectation that unique solutions can be demonstrated conclusively. That is far less often the case than Western rationality has tended to assume. We shall see.

As I have already implied, grouping items together and sorting them into separate contrasting bundles are inherent features of all language use. A hostile critic of that first book of mine used just that point to suggest that my whole endeavour was futile (Hamlyn 1968). What was my problem and what was the pay-off from my discussion when – according to this critic – there was no way in which Greek thought could fail to make use of analogies and polarities? If I had chosen to reply (which I did not), the first thing I would have said would have been that the particular analogies and polarities the ancient Greeks focused on, and how they used them, are significant. Some of them are distinctive to Greece and the prominent ones that were favoured tell us much about the ontological and even ethical presuppositions that their authors entertained, as well as about the scientific theories they wanted to put forward. Extending the point across cultures and periods, we can see that we can examine salient similarities and contrasts to explore such presuppositions more generally and to ponder the differences that such an examination reveals. We do not necessarily expect extensive cross-cultural universals in ethics. That has always been contentious. But not to find them in ontology challenges the robustness of some assumptions about the external reality we confront. Again I shall be exploring which assumptions about reality in general and its intelligibility can be said to be well grounded.

Secondly, the amount of self-conscious analysis that the Greeks themselves engaged in is in certain respects exceptional. If they used analogies and polarities repeatedly, both in particular explanations and theories and in general cosmological ones, they were, some of them at least, critical of their use. Their analyses of the weaknesses of these modes of thought prompted some of them to propose alternative, stricter, ideals of reasoning, which was where some of our Western preoccupations originated.

Persuasions were not good enough: demonstrations were needed. Metaphor was suspect: literality and univocity were demanded. However, reference to another society that also engaged in criticisms of misleading analogies and the like shows that the reaction that some ancient Greeks had was not the only possible one. Some prominent ancient Chinese thinkers also expressed their reservations about deceptive similarities, but without proposing the radical solutions that were favoured by Plato and Aristotle, echoes of which then reverberated down the centuries in European thought, with one writer after another demanding not just the likely, but the certain.[2]

But to those two points I would now add a third, namely that the very feature that my critic pointed to as obvious – the inevitable inherent use of similarities and contrasts in language – itself raises problems concerning the consequences that such a feature has for the limits of human under-standing and mutual intelligibility. Of course we are not limited to the generalisations suggested by the genera and species already picked out in whatever natural language we use. We can expose some terms as ambiguous or confused and we can coin others to capture the groupings we need to encapsulate new knowledge. But how is any one view about what is there to be sorted, and about how to do the sorting, to be validated against others? That is one of the key topics to be investigated in the studies that follow, and to suggest a possible way ahead, I shall rely on two concepts, on the one hand the notion of the multidimensionality of reality, and on the other that of the semantic stretch of the terms we use to capture it. I shall elaborate in due course, but for now may note first that recognising that reality is multidimensional allows for a plurality of accounts, each dealing with a different aspect or dimension of the subject-matter, thereby bypassing the usual dilemma that insists on a choice between 'realism' and 'relativism'. As for 'semantic stretch', this is proposed as an alternative to the literal/metaphorical dichotomy, where it offers, I would claim, two

---

[2] To mention just a single example, in the Port Royal logic (1996 [1683]: 239f.) Arnauld and Nicole set out three general rules which they find in the first place in geometry, namely not to leave any ambiguity in terms, basing reasoning only on clear and evident principles, and proving demonstra-tively all the conclusions put forward. They went on to gloss the first rule in an even stronger form: 'Leave no term even slightly obscure or equivocal without defining it.' It is striking that when the authors turn to 'what we know by faith' (260), they claim that this other kind of knowledge is 'often no less certain, nor less evident in its own way', namely knowledge derived from authority. So the mysteries of faith, such as the Trinity, the Incarnation and the Eucharist, so far from being an affront to human reason, just demonstrate its limitations and inability to understand the infinite extent of God's power. They quote Augustine on how what is new, strange and contrary to the course of nature may be a sign of its 'greatness, marvellousness, divinity', and so be 'more true, certain and enduring' (261). On the other side, the attempts, from the late 1950s on, by Perelman and others (e.g. Perelman and Olbrechts-Tyteca 1969) to redress the balance and restore the place of rhetoric in argumentation have been only partially successful.

advantages: first in that it represents the differences as a matter of degree as opposed to exclusive alternatives, and secondly in that it allows the possibility that every term may have some stretch, even, at the limit, those deemed to be univocal. That is not to say (as some have argued) that there is a metaphorical element in the use of every term, nor to collapse the literal into the metaphorical by treating the former as a null class. Rather it is to overhaul the terms in which the issue is formulated and to reject the alternatives, *either* literal *or* metaphorical, *either* strict *or* derived.

My first study starts with the problem of translation across languages, which as I have already remarked is just one aspect of the much larger questions of mutual intelligibility and of the possibilities of understanding in any context. The issue takes on a particular urgency in the light of recent anthropological debate: just how far is it possible to overcome the barriers to mutual understanding set up not just by different natural languages, but by radically different experiences of being in the world? When faced, as often, by such fundamental differences, how can we begin to grasp and interpret what is going on? If we use our existing conceptual framework will that not lead to distortion? But how can we fail to use that framework? The question turns on the extent and the nature of possible revisions to our initial assumptions.

My second chapter turns to comparatism: that is, not just the first-order activity of doing some comparing, but the second-order study of how comparisons in general are used, their functions and their multiple valences. Here too the problem of understanding the radical Other takes centre stage: here too the question is how to avoid turning the activity of comparing into a distorting exercise in reductionism. How can we make the most of what comparison can teach us?

Chapter 3 begins by taking a particular subject-area, namely ethics, and particular analogies proposed by two groups of thinkers in ancient China and Greece, to examine the tension between the recurrent appeal to images, models and the like, and the recognition of their inconclusiveness. Did the thinkers in question see this as an inevitable flaw in all ethical reasoning, or aim to devise ways of circumventing their shortcomings? What should we conclude about the strengths and weaknesses of analogical argumentation, not just in ethics, but in any field of investigation? On the one hand, the hazards of such argumentation are often obvious. On the other, we can question whether the remedies that have been proposed do not suffer from as many disadvantages as what they purport to replace.

That takes me, in turn, in Chapter 4, the core of the whole book, to study analogy as heuristic and to review the relations between images and argument more generally. Again I shall use the rich materials from ancient

Greece and China to examine these questions, but will add data from other ancient and modern societies, where a preoccupation, even an obsession, with resemblances, signs, signatures has often been diagnosed as a principal source of error.[3]

The justification for this focus on Greece and China here and elsewhere is two-fold. On the one hand, Aristotle was responsible for some of the radical ideas that went to create that European legacy I have spoken of, and we can examine the context and the circumstances in which he introduced them. On the other, we can test hypotheses concerning the general viability of his analyses against another culture that shared some of the preoccupations of the ancient Greeks but reacted to them very differently.

Of course we have to be aware of the limitations of our methods. We cannot experiment on the ancient Greeks and Chinese, nor plot the psychological and cognitive developments of particular individuals. We cannot match those kinds of studies which form the core of much modern developmental psychology and ethology (e.g. Gelman and Byrnes 1991, Carey 2009). But even taking just two ancient societies we can throw light on problems in cognition that continue to occupy researchers not just in cognitive science, but also in anthropology and philosophy. In the background lie the twin issues of the commonalities, and the specific variations, in human reasoning and argument.[4]

While each of those four chapters focuses on the knowing subject, Chapter 5 considers the issues from the side of the target subject-matter that

---

[3] Mill (1875 [1843]: book v, ch. 3, para. 8) identified as 'the most deeply-rooted perhaps' of all fallacies that 'the conditions of a phenomenon must, or at least probably will, resemble the phenomenon itself'. To illustrate this he cited (somewhat inaccurately) the version of the Doctrine of Signatures in Paris (1875: 47 [not 43–5]). This put it that 'every natural substance which possesses any medicinal virtues, indicates, by an obvious and well-marked external character the disease for which it is a remedy, or the object for which it should be employed'. But he went on to give examples of the fallacy from Bacon, Erasmus, Darwin, Leibniz and Descartes (in that order). Yet although Mill rejected Aristotelian complete induction, he proposed what he called the Methods of Agreement and of Difference as the two primary means of securing invariable laws of nature (book iii, ch. 8). The first proceeds by comparing together different instances in which the phenomenon occurs, the second by comparing instances in which the phenomenon does occur with instances in other respects similar in which it does not. I shall be returning to these issues in Chapter 4.

[4] Despite their common concern with aspects of human reasoning, the methods and goals of the historian and the developmental psychologist are, of course, quite distinct. The historian does not undertake controlled experiments to assess the development of cognitive skills in children and even in infants (assuming their attention span gives access to their notions of the normal and the unexpected). While cognitive scientists can aim to discover patterns of development that are valid cross-culturally (even though in practice their subjects are generally drawn from groups who are far from typical of human populations as a whole, see Henrich, Heine and Norenzayan 2010), the historian has to pay attention to the divergences in the practices of reasoning and in the explicit evaluations of such as between different groups as also between different individuals within them. Their modes of reasoning will reflect specific features of how they see the problems, their ambitions to achieve understanding and their notion of what it will take to convince others of their point of view.

is there to be known. The West, as already noted, has generally entertained robust notions on that subject. Natural science studies nature and the underlying assumption is that nature is universal, while human cultures differ. But as recent ontologically oriented anthropologists, such as both Descola and Viveiros de Castro, have insisted, that pair of presuppositions is itself far from universal. At the opposite end of the spectrum of possibilities, the assumption of a mononaturalism combined with multiculturalism is replaced by monoculturalism (what is shared by all living beings, and not just humans, is some culture) with multinaturalism: what distinguishes different living beings is precisely their natures, their physicalities, their bodies.

This evidently poses perhaps the biggest challenge that usual Western ontologies face. The fundamental problem is easily stated. Has the idea of a single reality there to be investigated to be abandoned? How can it be? While much of this debate hinges on the often contested interpretation of anthropological fieldwork, on which of course I can only comment as an outsider, again it seems possible to offer some clarification of the issues from my perspective as a comparativist historian and philosopher. While the anthropologist Descola identifies as just one possible ontological regime what he labels 'analogism', how does that relate to, is it even possible to reconcile it with, the findings of my previous chapters concerning analogies as a mode of thought?

Starting from the logical point that the apprehension of similarities and differences is fundamental to any attempt to classify phenomena or to make sense of experience, we must recognise that analogies are present in every ontology. So the question is not can we do without analogies (we cannot) but rather how to evaluate those we explicitly propose or implicitly rely on, how to sift those that are fit for purpose from those that are liable to mislead. But fit for whom, we have to ask, and for what purpose – questions that immediately implicate values, our own and other people's. There is evidently no neutral way of judging these, but that does not mean we have to, or should, or even can, simply avoid judgement altogether. Analogies are always fallible, but if their deceptiveness must put us on our guard, their potentiality to open up new perspectives offers us the best means of learning how to be self-critical.

A final chapter returns to the set of problems I identified at the outset of this introduction and takes stock of the main theses I have proposed. Wherein lie the true strengths and weaknesses of the Western legacy? Which notions turn out to need to be overhauled or used only with considerable reservations and qualifications? Which have proved their enduring worth?

What have very different traditions to teach us? Certainly they are a valuable resource to examine critically aspects of our normal assumptions that we usually take for granted. But where does that leave us on the crucial question of how to go about achieving greater understanding, of one another and of the world we inhabit? Without attempting to propose any sovereign remedies for the dilemmas we face, I hope to achieve some clarification of both types of issue, where again analogies in particular may serve not just as a warning but also as a guide.

While many critics have warned against the dichotomising tendencies that have been so prevalent in Western thought, I here offer specific objections with regard to realism and relativism, nature and culture, and the literal and the metaphorical in particular. That is the negative aspect of my discussion. Positively, by contrast, my chief recommendation, over and above my advocacy of the multidimensionality of reality and the semantic stretch of terms, is to make the most of comparisons, images, analogies, recognising that they may mislead, but sensitive also to the important insights they may give access to, not least when our comparisons lead us deep into the interpretation of radically different cosmologies and solutions to how we should live our lives. If we learn to understand our dependence on analogies, images and the like, and to appreciate how inappropriate quests for certainty may be, we may have a better chance to understand others, and indeed ourselves, as well as to learn from them how to expand our own intellectual and imaginative horizons. By understanding analogy better, the hope is that we shall be able to understand ourselves and one another more sympathetically.

In each case, the ideas I develop here were originally formulated as contributions to workshops and symposia, in Cambridge, London, Paris, Berlin, Berne and Madrid, or to special numbers of periodicals (*Journal of Cognition and Culture, HAU*), and in several instances those ideas pick up and develop points from my earlier publications. The fact that certain guiding threads, centring largely on the topic of analogy, linked those contributions, prompted me to attempt this synthesis. Finally I must remark that the end product has benefited greatly first from my audiences and commentators when I have tried out my ideas in provisional form in the circumstances I have just mentioned, and then from four helpful anonymous readers for Cambridge University Press. None of these is likely to agree with all my claims, but each of them contributed to the outcome by making me clarify my arguments.

CHAPTER I

On the very possibility of mutual intelligibility

My opening study poses the basic issue that any attempt at cross-cultural exploration faces, namely how, and how far, mutual understanding is possible, an issue of some urgency when we encounter what at first sight appear to be radically counter-intuitive beliefs. I shall begin by offering some reminders of the difficulties that even those who speak the same natural language encounter, before turning to the far more severe problems raised both by the ethnographic data and by ancient history. In the former case I shall propose some preliminary comments on recent anthropological debate, especially with regard to Descola's ontological schemata and Viveiros de Castro's perspectivism. In the latter my examination of the explicit arguments for which we have evidence especially, though not exclusively, from ancient Greece, will prompt me to suggest where we need to be wary of several of our own basic presuppositions. These concern the concept of nature, for example, and the view that if we do not adhere to a realist account we are thereby committed to a form of relativism that precludes mutual intelligibility. My controversial suggestion, where nature is concerned, is that it is itself a cultural artefact. On the second question, I argue that we can avoid that fateful dichotomy (realism/relativism) by factoring in the multidimensionality of reality. The upshot is not, of course, some way of guaranteeing success in understanding, but to remove some of the obstacles felt to stand in its way and to see some of the difficulties that undeniably remain as challenges to us to improve our understanding rather than as evidence that this cannot be done. The relevance of this to my study of analogies is, of course, that mutual intelligibility is necessary if comparison is to be possible.

Like the ethnographer, the student of ancient societies is faced with a recurrent problem of translation, and in one important respect suffers from an obvious considerable disadvantage. Modern ethnographers can question members of the groups they study to get some reaction on the question of whether or how well they have understood them, though the quality of the response will reflect the relationship the ethnographer has been able to build up. He or she may be told, simply out of politeness, how brilliantly he or she has grasped the meaning of their words and of their actions. The ancient historian is just confronted by documents and texts, those that have survived the vagaries of transmission and mostly now buried beneath a pile of earlier interpretations.

In both cases we have to be realistic about the level of understanding that can be achieved. But we have also to be realistic about the level of understanding attainable even when the conditions are optimal, when we are dealing with someone who shares with us the same natural language, maybe also the same upbringing and environment. The particular problems of trying to grasp the meaning of some ancient text in a foreign language, or the work of an author as a whole, are mirrored, even if less severely, in our efforts to understand some writing in English. What is it to say that we have grasped the meaning of King Lear, let alone of Shakespeare as a whole, or, to come down to today, of Salman Rushdie or A. S. Byatt? To state the obvious, it is never the question of 'the' meaning, just the one, but usually of multiple meanings. The point is familiar from religious hermeneutics, and although in that context we may sometimes suspect deliberate mystification, the lesson that readings are open-ended is surely obvious across the board: not even scientific communications are immune to multiple interpretations.

But if being realistic means we have to acknowledge difficulties, it also means that we should not be unduly pessimistic. One important point about translation and about understanding in general is that, although always difficult and always imperfect, it is seldom the case that we have to admit to complete and utter defeat. That is the case even with terms that are admitted to have no exact single equivalent in any but the natural language in which they occur, like German *Gemütlichkeit*, or Welsh *hwyl*, or Russian *toska* or Ifaluk *fago*, where we can get at least some inkling of what they cover.[1] No ethnographer returns from the field to say that he or she understood nothing of the society that was the subject of investigation. No student of ancient Greek philosophy admits to understanding Plato not at all. It is only if we have no grasp whatsoever of a particular language that we must admit to total incomprehension, of the words at least, and even then the body language of our interlocutors may leave us in little doubt about some of their feelings.

---

[1] The opacity of those last three terms was discussed in Lloyd (2007a: ch. 4).

What the first line of the *Daodejing* means, *dao ke dao fei chang dao*, has been the subject of countless commentaries down the ages in many different languages.[2] But if you have some classical Chinese, you will know, for instance, that *dao* can mean not just 'way', but also 'guide', that is show as the way. So while the first *dao* is 'the Way', with all its multiple associations, the second *dao* can be taken as 'shown as a *dao*' so that the whole says very roughly 'the Way that can be spoken of as a way is not the constant way'. The constant (*chang*) Way is thereby contrasted with others that fail that requirement of constancy, *because* they can be spoken of. That illustrates what an approximate translation can be like, with the added bonus, perhaps, of the substantive message to do with (in)expressibility, that this particular famous line conveys.

We can study the range of usage of *dao* and that of *chang*. At that point some might attempt to cordon off 'literal' from 'metaphorical' uses. But as I have already said, that is one of the dichotomies that cannot be taken for granted.[3] My preferred alternative is to make use of the notion of 'semantic stretch' which has the advantage that it allows that every term may have some stretch. *Dao* may be exceptional: there is a *Dao* of butchery and even one of robbery, though it is the *Dao* of the sages to which one aspires. Yet it is as well to make allowance for potential stretch in every term in any communicative exchange and that is even before we factor in further complex points from the pragmatics of the situation. When a live conversation is in question, there is, as noted, the body language of the speakers to consider and again the relationships between them, of friendship or hostility, cooperativeness or competitiveness, superiority or deference.

That may seem to open up an infinite number of options for interpretation, far beyond anything that Wittgenstein contemplated when he deployed the notion of 'family resemblances', although semantic stretch

---

[2] The *Daodejing* is a composite text which existed in several different variants in the second century BCE, as is proved by copies that have been found in excavated tombs that date from that period. I briefly discussed the interpretation of this first line in what became the standard version in Lloyd (2002: ch. 5).

[3] I analysed the historical background to the introduction of the literal/metaphorical dichotomy in Lloyd (1990: ch. 1), pointing out the importance of Aristotle's role in this. Scholars who have assumed that the classical Chinese must have had an equivalent to the concept of the 'metaphorical' often cite the notion of *yu yan* or 'lodge sayings' in *Zhuangzi* 27 (The *Zhuangzi* is a compilation mostly dating from between the fourth and second centuries BCE). But that, I argued in Lloyd (2002: ch. 5), is clearly mistaken. *Yu yan* belongs to a suggested trichotomy of ways of using speech (the other two being 'heavy sayings' and 'spill-over sayings') and neither of those two individually, nor both of them taken together, provide anything like the equivalent of a category of the 'literal'. Diagnosing the 'literal/metaphorical' dichotomy as in origin the product of Aristotelian polemic, I suggested 'semantic stretch' as an alternative in the same chapter.

shares with that notion the idea that we can trace similarities across a spectrum of meanings for any given term. Wittgenstein's most famous example of 'family resemblance' was in connection with 'games' where we should not forget his influential introduction of the concept of 'language games' in particular (Wittgenstein 1953: para. 66ff.). Semantic stretch, so far from precluding progress in understanding, may even be a necessary condition for it. The possibilities in interpretation are not limitless, even with the *Daodejing*, but they are liable to be prematurely circumscribed if we start from the assumption that there is just the one, correct, understanding that will be secured once we have identified the correct single 'literal' meaning and issued caveats concerning metaphorical uses. We must acknowledge that much always escapes us, but that does not mean that we must always remain in a state of complete bafflement. Reminding ourselves that we may have got it wrong is always salutary, but should encourage us to renew our efforts rather than simply give up in despair. This is of course what we naturally do, at least when we are not inhibited by some sense that we must be able to resolve the philosophical issues before we can even start.

Texts look as if they ought to say something that we shall have some opportunity to construe in other terms even if that may involve heavy paraphrasing. But what about pieces of music, works of art, ritual performances? We should not say that they do not signify anything, even when, as often, they do not refer. But to begin to put into words what we believe them to signify is always difficult, often seemingly impossible. What Beethoven's Fifth Symphony meant for the different members of the audience that E. M. Forster described as listening to it in *Howards End* is expressed, in that novel, in what now seem rather jejune terms. But in any case what a piece of music means for one person on one occasion is never going to be precisely what it means for another on that occasion, or even for the same person on a different occasion. Again the hermeneutic temptation is to elide all that diversity to get at some essential, core, understanding, but to do so is always going to be reductionist, always going to miss the opportunity to explore other possible resonances and associations.

Warnings as to the difficulty and imperfection of understanding are always needed, but it is amazing how much we *can* understand, including across different languages and dealing with unfamiliar subject-matter. We should never underestimate the capacity of humans to learn and to adapt, even in the face of pressures that urge us to stay with the views and practices of our elders and betters. Sure, we sometimes delude ourselves that we are on the right track. Sure, we are sometimes the victim of deliberate deception on the part of our interlocutors. But that would not be possible, if there was *always* deception. Our default assumption is that we are not being deliberately misled by our partners in conversation. Obscurantism in turn is only recognisable by contrast with the relatively plain and clear. The very fact that, with the help of an interlocutor, or just on our own, we can improve our grasp of what is being communicated, and correct some of our misunderstandings, should encourage us to continue our efforts, including even in the face of an insistence, on the part of those interlocutors or the apparent message of a text, that what we are dealing with is the inexpressible. *Dao ke dao fei chang dao* takes away with one hand, but gives us something with the other.

It is true that some aspects of modern philosophical discussion of the problems have not helped as much as they might. Quine's inscrutability of reference, which I mentioned in my introduction (Quine 1960), and Kuhn's incommensurable paradigms (Kuhn 1970) certainly underline the difficulties.[4] But we can concede that ultimately reference is inscrutable without conceding that it is hopelessly vague and arbitrary. Even if there is always an element of indeterminacy, we can narrow down the possibilities by a process we may compare to bracketing – in particular by excluding what lies outside the brackets. There was no ostrich on the scene when our friend announced 'gavagai', while there was indeed a rabbit, so it is less likely that 'gavagai' has to do with an ostrich let alone temporal ostrich slices than with something to do with rabbits, even though it may not be the creature in mind, but rather the event, or again it may be neither. Even when a rabbit event occurs, there are always plenty of other items and occurrences in the scene that may have occasioned the comment. Faced with the first exclamation 'gavagai' the outsider will be baffled: sufficient repetition of the word should get the process of bracketing under way. Similarly I learned to recognise Welsh 'hwyl' (roughly, inspired speech) by being exposed to it on many occasions and registering that people acknowledged it in some speakers but not in others, in some performances, but not in others.

As for Kuhn's incommensurabilities, they do not preclude, but may even presuppose, the possibility of comparison, where at least we can make a start. There is no common measure for the side and the diagonal of a square. But we can certainly say that the diagonal is longer than the side. It is only if both are recognised as lengths that we can say they are incommensurable. We do not bother to remark that there is no common measure between a

---

[4] The philosophical literature on the problem of reference is, of course, immense. It is not my aim here, nor in Chapter 2, to discuss aspects of this beyond their relevance to what I may call the anthropological issues of translating between languages and understanding other cultures.

length and a colour, for that involves a straightforward category mistake.[5] Paradigm shifts always pose tough problems of interpretation, especially when the same term, say 'force', or 'weight', or 'mass', comes to be used with quite new senses and referents. But in the stock historical instances used to illustrate such shifts we should not say there was total lack of comprehension between the parties. Copernicus certainly had a fair grasp of Ptolemy's astronomical system, Galileo of Aristotle's idea of natural motion, Einstein of Newton's classical dynamics, even when the definitions of key terms were being transformed and new ones had to be coined to convey the new understanding. Incommensurability issues a warning, but should not be thought to imply insoluble problems of comparability.

But while the ideas of Quine and Kuhn have often been construed as threatening to undermine mutual intelligibility, conversely other attempts to come to its defence likewise may suffer from shortcomings. Faced with such famous but much abused examples as the Nuer belief that twins are birds (Evans-Pritchard 1956) or the Dorze's that the leopard is a Christian animal (Sperber 1975), some adopt Davidson's hermeneutic principle of charity in interpretation (Davidson 2001), which recommends that what-ever statements are reported should be construed, so far as possible, as mak-ing sense in our terms.[6] Maybe we can find points of similarity between birds and twins, or between leopard behaviour and Christian behaviour, to see how the reported belief can be made to make sense, without our having to follow those interpreters who had recourse to some idea that the statements were not meant 'literally', but merely 'metaphorically'. Trying to decide between those two alternatives led to an impasse, the problem being compounded by the fact that the actors themselves, the Nuer and the Dorze, had no such explicit categories.

On the one hand, the supposition that those holding what seem to us counter-intuitive beliefs are just foolish or irrational obviously will not do as a general methodological principle. There are fools in every society, not excluding our own, but attempting to diagnose wholesale folly in whole communities is not just racist, but hardly compatible with their evident ability to survive, often in difficult circumstances, including many where the average urbanised citizens of 'advanced' industrial societies would

---

[5] To judge from the Mohist Canons (B 6, cf. Graham 1989: 416) already some ancient Chinese recognised that it is absurd to ask which is longer, a piece of wood or a night, and what there is more of, knowledge or grain. The texts associated with the fifth-century philosopher Mozi are a disparate collection put together between the fourth and the start of the first century BCE (Johnston 2010), with the Canons probably dating from around 300 BCE.

[6] For a recent review of the different ways in which the principle of charity has been taken, see Delpla (2001), referring to Davidson (2001). Cf. Forster (1998).

simply perish. Yet that of course is not to say that every custom and belief that is maintained in any human group is well adapted to the aims of survival or of flourishing. That would be straightforwardly to commit the functionalist fallacy. Nor is it to deny that cognitive psychologists such as Kahneman and Tversky have successfully identified many widespread errors in reasoning, especially when we are dealing with what they called 'judgement under uncertainty' (Tversky and Kahneman 1974, Kahneman, Slovic and Tversky 1982). One such is the so-called confirmation bias (studied also, for instance, by Evans 1989, Nickerson 1998, Mercier 2011 and Mercier and Sperber 2011), where more attention is paid to evidence that seems to support prior expectations than to other factors that do not.

But, on the other hand, the translation of Nuer or Dorze beliefs into terms that make sense according to our given categories presupposes that those categories are already up to the job, and there is no reason a priori to go along with that. Evans-Pritchard was a great ethnographer, but truth to tell some of his interpretations now reek of some of his own preoccupations, theological ones perhaps especially. Faced with those counterintuitive statements, whether in ethnography or in ancient texts, we may need to revise our own categories and understandings, quite substantially perhaps, on such matters as the notion of a person, for instance, or of agency and causation.[7] It cannot be assumed that our existing concepts will be adequate, and to do so is to miss the opportunities for learning that ethnography and the study of ancient societies both present. I believe my exposure to ancient Greek and Chinese ideas has taught me a thing or two. I shall give an example – nature – shortly.

Such general points are particularly germane to the recent – controversial – ontological turn in anthropology, to the explorations of radically different ontologies in Descola or of perspectivism in Viveiros de Castro, which I have already alluded to in the Introduction and to which I shall be returning in Chapter 5.[8] In the perspectivism of Viveiros de Castro

---

[7] Thus the concept of a person which was already problematised by Mauss (1938) has in recent years become even more contentious (e.g. Carrithers, Collins and Lukes 1985). What we might think of as stable individuals are sometimes seen as complexes of multiple relationships. Persons are not individuals, but, in the phrase introduced by Marriott (1976) made famous by Marilyn Strathern, 'dividuals', divisible into multiple components formed from relations with others and subject to constant disequilibrium (Strathern 1988, 1999, 2005, cf. Wagner 1991, Mosko 2010, Vilaça 2011). Different understandings of causal cognition were the subject of a collective volume, bringing together psychologists, anthropologists, philosophers and historians, edited by Sperber, Premack and Premack in 1995, although among the contributors a strongly universalist underlying position was maintained by, for example, Boyer, who argued (1995: 615) that 'causal judgements, however culturally variable, are constrained by a series of universal intuitive principles'.

[8] Latour's recent monograph (2013), stimulated in part by his reflections on the impasse of modernity, introduces further considerable possibilities for the exploration of multiple ontologies. The recent

it is not nature that is universal while cultures differ. Rather, all living beings share culture while their natures differ, so this is monoculturalism and multinaturalism as opposed to multiculturalism and mononaturalism. Moreover, the key categories that we might suppose to be given in nature – 'animals' and 'humans' among them – turn out to be inherently relational. For while humans see themselves as human, and animals as animals, and even spirits (if they see them) as spirits, animals see themselves as human and humans as animals whether as predators or prey (Viveiros de Castro 1998: 470–1; contested, however, by Turner 2009). This obviously has important repercussions not just for understanding what an 'animal' or a 'human' is, but also for how they should interact and behave in relation to one another – questions that no one who does not assume that we have already resolved all the problems of ecology can afford to ignore.

Descola (2013) invokes some of the same ethnographic data in defining what he calls 'animism', but that, for him, is only one of four different ontological regimes, varying according to the continuity or discontinuity they assume with regard to interiority (feelings of selfhood) and physicality (the material components of which things are made). Humans everywhere entertain some notions on these two topics, so they can be used to draw up a taxonomy of ontological regimes. To give a brief summary of that taxonomy, which I hope will suffice for my immediate purposes here, animism postulates a continuity between humans and other beings in interiority but a discontinuity in physicality (what differentiates humans and jaguars is the bodies they have, but both jaguars and humans have their own social relations and culture). Totemism, by contrast, postulates continuities on both counts (a human group and its totem share both physicality and interiority). Analogism (which Descola finds in both ancient Greece and China) is the reverse of totemism, assuming discontinuities both in interiority and physicality, but setting up networks of correspondences between humans and non-humans on both counts. Finally naturalism, which he plausibly suggests is the default ontology of modernity, supposes interiority to be divided and discontinuous (only humans have culture in the strict sense) but sees humans and non-humans as linked by their shared physicality: we are all made of the same stuff.

literature on the ontological turn comprises notable contributions, including some revisions of previously held views, by Pedersen (2011, 2012), Holbraad (2012), Laidlaw (2012), Heywood (2012), Laidlaw and Heywood (2012) and Holbraad, Pedersen and Viveiros de Castro (2014). Just how seriously this turn was meant to be taken has been called into question even by some of its proponents, as for example by Pedersen (2012), although elsewhere he joined forces with Holbraad and Viveiros de Castro to insist on its political implications in relation to empowering indigenous peoples (Holbraad, Pedersen and Viveiros de Castro 2014).

Descola uses his taxonomy to investigate divergent practices of giving, taking, exchanging, producing, protecting, transmitting. For decades now, to be sure, anthropologists have appreciated that these are far from straightforward interpersonal, say economic, transactions, for they carry fundamental implications for both intra- and inter-social relations. And Descola is able to show how different modes of those practices correlate with his diverse ontological schemata. Each schema underpins, and to that extent legitimises, a distinctive way of ordering social relations within and between human groups. While he speaks of his four schemata as 'ontologies', Severi (2013) has pointed out that they differ from the common philosophical usage of that term in being much looser and less explicit. Severi instances the Greek philosopher Parmenides who constructed a theory of being on the basis of the argument that what is cannot not be and who then deduced the characteristics of that being, notably its changelessness and timelessness. This can indeed be seen as inaugurating the long and diverse traditions of Western metaphysics with which we are familiar. By contrast, however, Descola's regimes are better thought of as ideal types (cf. also Taylor 2013). As Severi (2013: 195) put it, 'what is particularly interesting about them is precisely their unsystematic character, the fact that they always leave a space open for different strategies of thought' (cf. Lenclud 2013: 328ff., who also problematises the applicability of the term 'ontology'). This suggests that over a range of experience, and communication about that, there are no grounds to postulate or suspect a distinct ontology as such to be at work. But conversely we should not suppose that *our* ontological presuppositions (whatever they may be) are being assumed.

So we must certainly pay due attention to the degrees of systematicity and of explicitness in the material we are dealing with, ranging from fully articulated sequences of arguments to sets of tacit overarching assumptions, though if the latter may exhibit a certain vagueness about what there is, they can nevertheless express quite determinate rules about the proper ways of ordering relations, not just within human society but between humans and other living beings. However, what both the ancient Greek and the ethnographic data have in common is that they pose challenges to our common preconceptions in the first instance about such topics as agency, causation, substance, space and time, and indeed about morality. In such cases the problems of translation are especially acute, though to be sure similar issues arise also with many mundane, concrete terms and how they are to be understood.

Thus from the jaguar's perspective the blood of his prey (as we see it) is manioc beer. This controlled equivocation, as Viveiros de Castro

(2004) calls it, might appear to a naturalist completely to destabilise mutual understanding, across different human groups as well as across different living creatures, to the point where the only thing that might be understood is that the jaguar's perception is indeed radically different from 'ours', though that is not to say anything about what *his* understanding is, except that it appears that jaguars, like us, enjoy drinking 'beer'. Yet that is rather to miss the whole point of perspectivism, which is that both the sense and the referents of terms (including 'beer') shift across the languages of different kinds of creature, being relative to the creatures in question, in particular being determined by the bodies they have. Translation is then not a matter of finding equivalent words to convey information about a single world, but of identifying different worlds to which the same words apply.[9]

But how is the jaguar's perspective to be accessed? It is only shamans who are in a position confidently to pronounce on that, for they alone can cross species boundaries, which in turn means that what is taken for a jaguar may be a shaman in disguise, or vice versa. It is certainly not easy to know where you are. But that is precisely the fundamental message. Rather than conclude that this difficulty, for us, of accessing others' perspectives undermines the whole enterprise, we should reflect on what we can learn, for example, from considering what it would be for persons and substances to be relational, where we can start from, and use as a model, our familiar – banal – acceptance that the same individual can be both father (of one person), brother (of another) and son (of yet another), though in the perspectivist process 'the same individual' gets to be radically problematised. The Achuar and the Araweté and many other groups, not limited to Amazonia, hold that other beings beside themselves are defined by the culture, rituals, rules of exchange and so on that constitute their way of being in the world. But what each kind of being apprehends depends – so the claim is – on the bodies they have.

The same applies, these peoples would say, to the Whites who come to study them, for they (we) have the customs they (we) have because their (our) bodies are what they are. It is clear that the Achuar and the Araweté themselves puzzle over the Whites studying them. Indeed they can be said to do anthropology on the Whites as much as the Whites do anthropology on them, as Viveiros de Castro suggested in his *Métaphysiques cannibales*

---

[9] Vilaça (2013: 175–6) gives an example from her fieldwork among the Wari', where different individuals puzzled over what in jaguar language is meant by 'nao' (the name of a nut the Wari' enjoy eating). In the process they tried out various 'translations' before arriving at a satisfactory result. 'That's it: papaya is paca [for the jaguar].'

(2009).[10] But their anthropology does not presuppose the same common-alities and divergences as ours does, for to start with their commonalities relate to culture, their divergences to nature.

Descola's plurality of ontological schemata helps us to correlate different practices of exchange, sacrifice and other relations with corresponding regimes. But it too explodes any assumption of a privileged status for the naturalism that still dominates Western ideology and that presupposes a robust notion of the natures out there for us to be talking about. The relevance of that to my strategic interests in examining still current Western assumptions is obvious.

Translation across cosmologies or perspectives might then seem to be impossible, unless we are prepared (as many may not be[11]) to suspend adherence to our usual categories. That is the strategic problem this material poses and I shall come back to it later. But for now let me concentrate on the particular assumption that mutual intelligibility depends on there being a single nature for communication to be about. That of course is the modernist postulate. But should we go along it? Both Descola and Viveiros de Castro challenge the nature/culture dichotomy. Yet in suggesting how to go beyond it, both do so in terms that continue to use it.

Now I must recognise my own limitations in the face of the ethnographic aspects of the issues of translation raised by the 'ontological turn'. But I do not think it is impossible to bring to bear some historical points from my studies of ancient ontologies. At least my investigations of these prompts me to propose a different way of bypassing the treacherous dichotomy between nature and culture, which was of course what Descola's book set out to transcend and which was radically revised by Viveiros de Castro. My historical analysis of how the concepts of nature, *natura*, Greek *phusis*, originated in the West yields what may be a crucial point, namely that they

---

[10] As Schaffer in particular has pointed out (2010: 286–7; cf. Stocking 1995: 236) the trope of indigenous peoples doing anthropology on the anthropologists goes back to Rivers (1912), who imagined an 'idealised Melanesian' coming to much the same conclusion about 'us' as Lévy-Bruhl had reached concerning them. If Lévy-Bruhl spoke of their 'prelogicality', the Melanesians might have concluded that 'we' suffered from a 'postlogical mentality' (Rivers 1912: 402). The theme was taken up by Hocart (1915) in his criticisms of Marett (1912). Where Marett had written 'just as a dog lives in a world of smells that we cannot perceive, so the savage lives in a world of magico-religious influences and relations which we are apt to miss entirely' (Marett 1912: 252), Hocart, speaking on behalf of the imagined 'savages', substituted for the second clause 'so the White Man lives in a world of bacterio-medical infection and contagion that we cannot perceive'.

[11] Those I have in mind may be swayed by the thought that the problems only arise in connection with beliefs that they can easily dismiss as fanciful, and that for all necessary purposes they may remain confident in science and in the values that have underpinned the rise to hegemony of Western societies. It will be evident that such complacency is the prime target of my whole analysis.

were very much the product of a particular polemical situation, for which we have direct evidence in Greece.[12]

Those who went into battle, there, under the banner of *phusis*, were dubbed the *phusikoi* or natural philosophers (starting in the sixth century BCE, but becoming especially prominent in the next two centuries). They claimed 'nature' as the domain over which they were to be the acknowledged experts. Where traditionally in Greece such phenomena as earthquakes, thunder and lightning, eclipses and diseases had generally been assumed to be the work of the gods (they were not *natural* phenomena then), the *phusikoi* argued that that was a category mistake. It was to ignore that those phenomena had regular causes – natures, in fact– that could be investigated: and they, the natural philosophers, could supply the correct theories and explanations (though in fact many of those they proposed were quite fantastical). Where the traditionalists saw lightning and thunder as Zeus at work – to be probed for symbolic or even moral associations, not physical ones – the naturalists saw the clash of clouds or whatever. Where the traditionalists saw eclipses as omens, the naturalists said they were regular and predictable. We should note, in passing, that in this case we cannot say that the traditionalists and the naturalists saw what they saw because of the bodies they had: that illustrates where that particular interpretive move, which we owe to the ethnographers, will not do. We have to account for that difference of opinion, and the ones we are familiar with in our own debates, differently. We move into new contexts of intellectual and other rivalries and new modes of discourse, ones that depend heavily, most would say, on literacy and on a level of complexity of social organisation. More basically still Viveiros de Castro would insist that you cannot expect Greek – or Chinese – style pluralism in a human group numbering in their hundreds not their tens of thousands. The Araweté nowadays number under 400.

Yet reference to other ancient societies shows that literacy cannot be the whole answer. Ancient China had no single concept that covered what *phusis* covered in Greek or *natura* in Latin, and the same applies to every other ancient society with which I am familiar: Mesopotamia, Egypt, India, even though I know far less about them. The Chinese recognised the spontaneous as the spontaneous, heaven and earth as heaven and earth, the different characteristics that different creatures are born with as those characteristics, and so on. But they were not tempted to suppose that they

---

[12] My original proposal that 'nature' was invented (not discovered) by the ancient Greeks was first published in Lloyd (1991: ch. 18), though in earlier work (Lloyd 1973) I had indeed talked of a discovery.

were dealing with *the same problem* in all those different instances. They
had indeed different concepts in each of those contexts, speaking of *zi
ran* when discussing the spontaneous, of *tiandi* when talking of heaven
and earth, and *xing* when identifying the key characteristics of things. Nor
were they tempted to read off value judgements from 'nature' as such (as
many Greeks did), even though they certainly debated moral questions
and took different views on whether humans are inherently good, bad or
indifferent.[13]

Nature, I conclude, is not natural at all, but a cultural artefact,[14] as
much as a political regime or a set of religious beliefs and practices is. It
is culture that is common, in the sense that all human groups (and some
would say some animals) have *some* culture – and the humans generally
have some concept that expresses their sense of their own society and
its ways (though what that comprises is of course not unproblematic, as
has often been observed, for example, by Kroeber and Kluckhohn 1952,
Wagner 1975, Kuper 1999 and Levinson and Jaisson 2006). So culture, in
some understanding of that term, has a chance of being a cross-cultural
universal, while nature is culturally relative. That should release us from
any assumption that whatever people thought they were dealing with in
the physical world has to correspond to 'nature', has to be shoehorned into
our category, in other words. Of course some idea of the regularities in the
phenomena *is* universal. We rely on that to get by in everyday life, when
we plant crops or light a fire. But *which* phenomena they are, and how
exceptions are to be accounted for, are *questions* where we cannot assume
that an explicit concept of nature will always provide the answers. Besides,
regularity by itself does not imply 'natural', since many regularities belong
rather to the domain of the social or the cultural.

So when I say that nature is an invention, I am not just claiming that our
understanding of nature is. My claim is the much stronger one, that nature
itself is our construct, one we owe ultimately to our Greek legacy. If we hold
that nature is out there unproblematically waiting to be investigated, we
have simply not been critical enough of our own deep-seated assumptions.
We may think that everyone must be in command of an explicit category
of 'the natural', but that turns out to be *our observers'* concept, not a reliable
actors' one, though of course, as I have just said, those actors no doubt
have *some* idea that some phenomena are regular and that some objects

---

[13] There is a hard-hitting debate between Mencius, Gaozi and Xunzi on precisely that issue in the
fourth and third centuries BCE: see Graham (1989: 117ff.) and cf. below, Chapter 3.
[14] Others tackling the problems from other perspectives might agree with this conclusion, though
without depending, as I do, on a historical argument.

have stable characteristics. We tend to export our notions of 'natural kinds' far too uncritically. Confident that animals and plants (for instance) form such, we extend the concept across the board throughout what we still call the natural sciences. Yet even in the paradigmatic zoological and botanical instances, *which* groupings are to be identified depends upon weighting similarities and differences. Although there evidently *are* plenty of similarities and differences to refer to, some seemingly quite uncontroversial, when we probe more deeply, the question of which ones to privilege becomes problematic and indeed so too do the concepts of genus and species themselves, however well they may seem to serve us for those ordinary practical purposes of everyday life. So it turns out that our notion of 'nature' continues to be problematic, and its status as a cross-cultural universal, and as an analytic tool for the interpretation of ontologies, is further called into question.

Yet to my controversial views on these subjects there are at least two immediate objections. In fact Viveiros de Castro raised one, when he objected to my proposal on the grounds of its paradoxicality, in that it destroys the symmetry between the pair, nature and culture.[15] But that was part of the object of my exercise, as indeed he allowed.

The second objection is that I have shot myself in the foot. Without nature how can the external world be investigated or understood, or how can other ontologies be? Have I not thereby fallen out of the realist frying pan into a relativist fire? Again that is a dichotomy that I am not the only person thinks needs overhauling.

The way I recognise the pluralism in ontologies proceeds rather differently from Descola and Viveiros de Castro. I agree with them in rejecting the assumed privileged status of a naturalist ontology. But my brand of ontological pluralism and the way I avoid the realism/relativism dichotomy are a matter of what I call the multidimensionality of the phenomena, or, alternatively, the multidimensionality of reality.[16] It may seem shocking to consider those two formulations interchangeable. But the appearance/reality dichotomy is another one that needs to be pensioned off. In

---

[15] See Viveiros de Castro (2010) where he explored the 'multidimensionality of incommensurability'. One of his arguments (326) was that some notion of nature 'as anti-culture or extra-culture, the negative or the background of the self-image of the socius' should be admitted 'as a legitimate candidate to some sort of universality'. Yet given the variety in the understandings of 'culture', what is opposed to and distinguished from it, has, at best, only a proxy universality, for in some contexts that might approximate to 'nature' but in others to revealed truth or to divine law.

[16] I introduced 'multidimensionality' in my sense in Lloyd (2004: ch. 7). I discussed the problem of colour in particular, with some background information concerning earlier and ongoing controversies, in Lloyd (2007a: ch. 1).

many contexts what is real is what appears, and conversely, though to be sure appearances may deceive. But then reality too may hide. The more important point, in both cases, is the possible, indeed the likely, multidimensionality.

Let me cite one of my favourite examples, colour, to illustrate that multidimensionality. In that case, the three dimensions of hue, luminosity and saturation provide three different sets of differentiations although that point is not always taken into account, particularly by those on the hunt for cross-cultural universals. There is no one correct way to talk about colour. We should not privilege one of the three ways and exclude the other two. All three are valid, and indeed there is every chance that all three modes of differentiation are discriminable by humans in normal circumstances, and so it is a mistake to think we have to choose between them. That does not mean that this introduces ambiguities that preclude generalisation. It is true that a multidimensional phenomenon cannot be given a single *per genus et differentiam* definition. But it can and should be given a disjunctive account, where each of the disjuncts (in the colour case, hue, luminosity and saturation) can be identified unambiguously, though each has its particular considerable semantic stretch.

But if thus far my position is 'relativist', it is not at all relativist insofar as I recognise that in each case there are more or less correct ways of doing the differentiations. Colour talk is certainly not just arbitrary: it is not the case there (or anywhere else) that just anything goes, whatever Feyerabend may have claimed or have been represented as claiming with his 'anything goes' (Feyerabend 1975). Nor is it impossible to allow communication between different modes of colour talk, even though the particular vocabulary for the particular differentiations in view may be distinctive for that particular mode. Multidimensionality does not rule out mutual intelligibility. In this case it may even be a necessary condition for it.

The consequences for translation and understanding go like this. A vocabulary that simply differentiates hues will not by itself be up to the task of capturing the other two modes of differentiation. Thus far translation is not possible if we stick to that single vocabulary. But of course we do not need to do so. What we can use are complementary modes of discourse to do justice to all three dimensions of differentiation, yielding a more comprehensive understanding of the subject-matter – and our notions of what the subject-matter itself comprises will need to be modified as we discover its multidimensionality. But then there is nothing to prevent our conveying the complementary character of the phenomena in different languages, with more or less adequate translations between them. In some cases neologisms will be needed. In many cases the idiosyncratic range of particular existing colour terms in one language will need a gloss or a paraphrase, even quite an extended commentary, in another. The French 'brun' is an oddball and so too is 'blond' used of tobacco or beer, though of course the phenomenon is not confined to French: ancient Greek '*xanthon*' and '*chlōron*' (conventionally inadequately rendered as 'yellow' and 'green') are other examples, where *chlōron*, for instance, denotes what is fresh, unripe, full of sap (cf. Lyons 1995: 220).

Indeed in many cases what have been represented as colour terms turn out not to be so. Rather they are terms whose primary references have nothing to do with colour: they pick out, rather, the living from the dead, or the succulent from the dry.[17] Within a single natural language, shifts between one register and another, and other possible sources of ambiguity, will occur. But at least we shall not be driven, as the former British Prime Minister W. E. Gladstone thought he was driven, from the observation that many ancient Greek colour terms relate to luminosity to conclude that they may all have been colour-blind and unable to distinguish hues (Gladstone 1877). He never read, or if he read, he ignored, Aristotle on the rainbow.

Where, I may now ask more generally, do my suggestions leave the epistemology of anthropology or of ancient history? Does the ontological turn in anthropology spell the demise of its epistemology, as some have thought (Henare, Holbraad, Wastell 2007, Holbraad 2012), leaving us perhaps with the conclusion that epistemologies are relative to the distinctive ontologies in play? Once again that gestures towards a conclusion of mutual unintelligibility. But once again that may be resisted.

It is true that the traditional dichotomies or dualisms within epistemology, between reason and perception, or between the a priori and the empirical, once again exhibit their limitations if considered as alternatives. But the correct response is not to abandon both sides of each pair, nor to plump for one to the exclusion of the other, but to combine them. That corresponds to my own practice here, for on the one hand I have been discussing what understanding is possible on the basis of an abstract analysis, but on the other I do that with as much attention as I can manage to empirical case histories which can act as a check on where the analysis needs correcting and complexifying. Epistemology, on this view, is not the bogey-man it has been represented as being by those who suspect that

---

[17] This was a point that, following Lyons (1995), I argued against Berlin and Kay (1969) in Lloyd (2007a: ch. 1), citing Conklin's original report of Hanunoo 'colour' terms (Conklin 1955).

it is merely a covert way of denying others' claims to know. The multi-dimensionality of what is there to be known cannot help but generate a multidimensionality of ways of knowing.

But several possibly fundamental objections to my use of those notions of multidimensionality and of semantic stretch must now be met to conclude this discussion. First it might be argued that I am still trapped in my own particular conceptual framework, even that everyone always is. Is it not the case that others' categories either will be reduced to mine, or will forever remain beyond reach? Of course my particular conceptual resources are whatever they are at any moment in time (though I can see they have changed over time, as I said). But my answer to that first question would be to reject the alternative. Provided I am indeed allowed the point that conceptual frameworks (like languages themselves) are revisable, reductionism can be avoided.

Then a second objection might be that I am somehow presupposing some transcendent meta-language into which all others can be parsed, which surely savours of Western hegemonic pretensions: give me a place to stand and I can move the world. Again I would resist, for I would claim both that I allow a voice to each pluralist rendering of multidimensionality, and that I recognise the revisability, and of course the imperfections, of my own understanding. A single meta-language, let alone one that imposes a rule of strict univocity, is a chimera; rather we can and should exploit the full resources of every understanding to which we can have access, and that will include those expressed in actions rather than words.[18]

I am reminded of a Chinese story in *Zhuangzi* about carpenter Bian.[19] He had the cheek to reprimand his employer, Duke Huan, for reading old books. The Duke protests: 'What business is it of a carpenter to criticise what I read? If you can explain yourself, well and good, but if not, you die.' Whereupon Bian refers to his own work as a carpenter. When he makes a wheel, if he chips at the wood too slowly the chisel does not grip: but if too fast, it jams and catches the wood. The right way to do it is something he feels in his hands and his heart responds, but he cannot put it into words. 'That is how you become expert at chipping wood, while the books of the past are just dregs.' In such a case the feeling is the understanding.

However, even if we reject the notion of a single stable meta-language the problem does not go away, indeed it might be thought to be aggravated

---

[18] Again this point was emphatically made by Wittgenstein (1953), and has been taken up by many others, notably by Ingold (2000) and the contributors to Henare, Holbraad and Wastell (2007).

[19] *Zhuangzi* 13 (cf. Graham 1989: 187). The story also appears in *Huainanzi* 12: 9b–10a, another compilation, this one assembled under the auspices of Liu An, king of Huainan, in 139 BCE.

by that rejection. How, I asked, is any translation *across* cosmologies to be achieved? It is all very well, some will say, to insist that reality is multidimensional and that every term may exhibit some degree of semantic stretch, but how does that bridge the gulf between divergent perspectives? If we reject the realist option, according to which only one ontology is correct, and the others must be dismissed as mistaken, are we not forced (once again) to the relativist view, according to which not only should we say all are correct, but also that there is no neutral way of judging them?

Once again that dichotomy obstructs a resolution. The multidimensional move would have it first that each ontology deals with a particular manner of ordering reality, including the key considerations of interiority and physicality. Secondly, each may do so in a more or less satisfactory, and certainly not arbitrary, way. But more or less satisfactory to whom? In the first instance, of course, to the actors themselves, to the Achuar and the Araweté and to all those others whose cosmologies have been explored by the ethnographers, where we must allow, with Severi, that some are more comprehensive and more explicit, more like philosophical ontologies indeed, than others.

But it is then up to observers, to us, to see what we can learn from the exercise of investigating their ways of being in the world, assuming, as before, that we do not claim that we have all the answers we need already. That means suspending judgement on all sorts of issues and being prepared to revise much of what we normally take for granted about those key concepts of person, agency, causation, space, time and, yes, certainly, nature. Clearly we must abandon the assumption that reality is a given, to which unmediated access is possible. Yet neither actors nor observers will settle for 'anything goes'.

But then does that not amount to some wishy-washy politically correct liberal relativism? Not if we can still provide for the possibility of diagnosing error in ourselves and others, allowing that each of those is tricky – for different reasons, for we may be insufficiently self-critical in the first case, and may not have got to the bottom of what is at stake in the second.[20] But evidently we are not infallible; no more was any given ancient Greek or Chinese thinker, no more are present-day Achuar or Araweté. But before concluding that we or they have made a mistake, we have first to ensure that we have done our best to explore the complexities of interpretation that I have been talking about, and there may always be an element of doubt

---

[20] I shall consider in Chapters 5 and 6 some examples where error may be diagnosed, though I shall duly observe how that judgement is often complicated by problems of translation: that is, with determining the senses and referents of the terms in question.

about how thorough that exploration has been. In many cases we may say it can never be complete: but in some simple ones it is certainly possible to draw a line and reassure ourselves that the job has been adequately done for the occasion in question. We have to get on with our everyday transactions, and indeed we do so.

Of course it is up to other researchers, not just ethnographers and ancient historians, but also linguists, cognitive scientists, evolutionary psychologists, to react to these proposals. I attempt no general theory of translation, of course, let alone a general formula for how mutual understanding is possible. But I offer these thoughts as suggestions about what can reasonably be expected and about how one can go about the task. The very open-ended character of translation may look to be a menace to mutual intelligibility, but that is only so if we hanker after definitive renderings. Abandoning that will-o'-the-wisp, we can rather welcome that open-endedness as a positive resource for increasing understanding. My next problem is to probe further the underlying assumptions in the type of comparativist endeavour on which I have embarked.

CHAPTER 2

The multiple valences of comparatism

By 'comparatism' I understand not the first-order activity of making comparisons, but rather the second-order one of analysing how comparisons are used. This, to be sure, will largely be a matter of comparing how comparisons have been used, especially those that juxtapose some 'other' with some 'us', though we shall see that the motivations for so doing can differ widely. Then a second problem that comparatism raises relates to the validity or the justification for any such activity of comparing. What indeed are the criteria for viable comparisons? Should comparing be limited to those cases where we can specify a clear *tertium comparationis*? And how is that to be defined and who gets to settle that? Again, against those who assume that it is a normal, indeed an inevitable, resource for human understanding, there have been those who seek to impose strict controls on its use or even to replace it by what is represented as a more secure brand of argumentation. That last is a topic I shall take up in Chapters 3 and 4.

However, for now my chief aims are two-fold, first to uncover the hidden and sometimes not so hidden agenda that comparatism often serves, notably to suggest the superiority of one group's views – religious, cosmological, ethical – by way of a demonstration, or at least an assertion, of the inferiority of alternatives. That will take me, secondly, to an examination of whether the typical prejudices of comparatism can be overcome and, if so, how. Any analysis, such as those I am undertaking in these studies, must be based on a particular natural language into which others' ideas are parsed, with the evident danger that that will more or less distort them by imposing inappropriate categories, such as no doubt, to some extent, the very ones I have just used, 'religious', 'cosmological', 'ethical'. But while there can be no entirely neutral viewpoint from which to assess contending opinions, that does not mean we have no option but to stay with our existing conceptual framework. I hope to clarify the room for manoeuvre available to us, and indeed I shall bring comparatism to bear to help resolve some of the problems. The paradoxical point I shall argue for is that the

29

very otherness of the Other, when we can get a hold of it, is a precious resource for us to broaden our intellectual and imaginative horizons.

There can have been very few human societies that have been totally isolated from all others and that know nothing of any other society. One problem here, so far as living societies go (dead ones are another matter, to be sure), is how anyone else can know about any such society, for as soon as contact is made with its members, that removes their total isolation. However, most human societies who know about others assume that they themselves provide the models of a proper human community, maybe the only authentic one, and that other groups all fall short. Ethnography provides countless examples where members of a particular society refer to themselves simply as 'the people' and do not accept the names that are given to them by others. As I have noticed before (Lloyd 2012a: 15), we do not need to travel to Amazonia or Siberia to find such. My own forebears, the Welsh, will do perfectly well, since we do not refer to ourselves as Welsh but as Cymru, the people, comrades.

But knowing about other peoples (as in the overwhelmingly majority experience) opens up a major problem. What to make of them? Are they truly humans at all? Where did they come from? When, as quite often, other animals are thought to have originally been humans, who then turned into animals, that provides a model that can be adapted to explain other humans, who accordingly might have quite different origins from 'us'. If we need one story for 'our' origin, whether that covers just us and not other humans, or also other humans, and perhaps also every living being, are going to be questions that will need answering. Fresh knowledge of other humans, and of the world we all inhabit, can disrupt assumptions about such origins, as happened in Europe when the Genesis story came to be seen to be flawed, both about the origins of the world and about those of other races. At the same time, the very otherness of other groups can serve to reinforce ideas about the proper way of organising social life, 'our' way, and so to make clearer who we are, what is distinctive about us and what makes us superior to those other people. Comparison thus inevitably separates the comparanda even while it finds, or presupposes, similarities between them.

The exploration of other societies and systems of belief has potentially multiple valences, five to be precise, which will provide the guiding threads for my discussion here. These differences will depend mainly on who controls the comparison and with what end in view. First, as already noted, comparatism can be used to claim superiority for the views and practices of those who are doing the comparing. Secondly, it can be employed rather to recognise the superiority of others' ideas, customs and achievements. Thirdly, the point may be rather to stress the commonalities between the comparanda. In all three of those cases it is assumed that those comparanda are intelligible. But in a fourth role for comparatism the Other is thought to be not just difficult to comprehend, but strictly incomprehensible.

This will take me back to the problems of mutual intelligibility discussed in the last chapter, but now we can identify a fifth valence, namely when what presents itself as radically different is construed not as a source of aporia, but as a resource for learning something new.[1] That will depend on giving an equal hearing to divergent perspectives on what is at stake. Stengers (2011: 56) has insisted with some force that no comparison is legitimate if the parties concerned are not each able to present their own view on what the comparison is about. She instances the myth versus science dispute originating in Greece, indeed, where the 'scientists' set out to disbar the mythical as if it was just botched science. Of course when we are dealing with the views of long-dead peoples, they cannot speak for themselves. All the more important then that we entertain the possibility that they construed what the comparison was about very differently from their opponents.

I shall start with what I have just identified as the second valence of comparatism, where knowledge of other societies, or what passes as such, is used not to put them down as inferior, but rather to recognise their impressiveness or even superiority. Many societies are reported as believing that their neighbours' shamans are far more powerful than their own (Shirokogoroff 1935: 373, 387ff.). The Other then becomes a source of ideas and practices to imitate and incorporate, though in the case of those shamans they may be something you have reason to be wary of, even to fear. Even so, they can provide a model by which your own local shamans can be judged. Contact with other peoples thus opens up space for reflection on and criticism of your own society, though how far that will be allowed depends on a whole lot of factors, political, religious, institutional.

However, comparatism is far more often used to confirm the superiority of the familiar over the exotic, 'our' beliefs and 'our' way of doing things, as opposed to 'theirs'. 'Their' different ways just confirm their inferiority. But what is 'our' way exactly? Is that a simple matter? Hardly. Most members of a community may entertain little doubt about certain core institutions and practices (we should, for example, practise monogamy and observe certain

---

[1] What I label the fifth valence differs from the second (the appreciation of the other's superiority) in that the object is not necessarily to valorise the other or the new in contradistinction to the given or what you already know about.

restrictions about whom we can marry and what we eat). But that leaves plenty of room for divergence at the periphery (how we should cut our hair or whether we should). That opens up the possibility that individuals or sub-groups may seek to criticise or condemn certain behaviour patterns and beliefs of others in their own society, by suggesting that they do not conform to the norms these particular individuals wish to impose on their fellows: they should not, but they do, cut their hair. Such improper behaviour and beliefs may be associated with outsiders, aliens, foreigners, even 'animals'. Reference to other groups – based on conceptions that may be largely imaginary – is then a handy but quite suspect way of trying to exercise control over fellow members of your own society.

Ancient societies provide plenty of examples. The situation of the ancient Greeks was exceptional in that they were familiar with two civilisations, Egypt and the Persian Empire, that it was difficult, or rather impossible, simply to dismiss. In fact they were in awe of both, of the architectural monuments they encountered in Egypt and of the general power and wealth of Persia. They had nothing to put besides those, and indeed recognised that in many ways they could not compete (the second mode of comparatism). But that did not stop them claiming their own superiority in other respects: for example, that they were truly free, not everywhere ruled by tyrants.[2] Eastern autocrats were paradigms of self-indulgence and luxury (the ancient Greeks invented 'Orientalism'), though the implicit contrast with Greek moderation was always difficult to sustain.

While Herodotus, for one, attempted to identify some Greek divinities with Egyptian ones (2.50ff.), knowledge – or what passed as such – of others' religious beliefs could be used with devastating effect, to criticise them and then indeed by extension some of the traditional views of the Greeks themselves. Polytheisms are generally better able to cope with others' gods than monotheistic regimes, but already in pagan antiquity the idea of gods and goddesses in human form was the subject of blistering attack. In the sixth century BCE Xenophanes suggested that the Ethiopians imagined their gods as black and snub-nosed, and the Thracians theirs as blue-eyed and red-haired (Fr. 16). More strikingly still, he extended the argument to non-human animals. 'If oxen and horses and lions had hands and could draw and fashion works as humans do, horses would draw the gods shaped as horses and lions as lions, making the bodies of the gods resemble their own bodies' (Fr. 15). That serves to undermine traditional anthropomorphic

---

[2] One notable expression of such an idea comes in the fifth-century BCE Hippocratic treatise, *On Airs Waters Places*, ch. 16.

views, Greek and non-Greek, pretty fundamentally, but his own preferred conception of the deity, 'in no way like mortals in body or in mind' (Fr. 23), still depends on an analogy and a difference. He [God] 'sees as a whole, perceives as a whole, hears as a whole' (Fr. 24). God is still like us, in seeing, perceiving and hearing, even if unlike us in not needing sense organs to do so.

Both Hebrew and Christian monotheisms made heavy use of pagan polytheism to point up the contrast between their own – different – ideas of the one true God and the false idols of the polytheists. Christianity in particular not only rejected Greco-Roman pagan anthropomorphism, but trumped all other notions about the similarity of God to humans with the figure of Christ, at once God and man.

To illustrate the problems such a belief brought in its wake, it is enough to consider its implications for some Christian missionary projects. The whole endeavour of Ricci and his fellow Jesuits to convert the Chinese to Christianity in the sixteenth century is a saga of misunderstandings on both sides together with some deliberate mystifications (Gernet 1985). When it became clear to the Chinese that the Christians worshipped a criminal who had been executed on a post in the shape of the Chinese graph for the number ten (+ in the Chinese numeral system) (a point that the Jesuits had tended to keep quiet about though they did insist Christ had died to save us from our sins), they reacted in dismay. Different Christian sects for their part attempted to make sense of the Chinese notions of Heaven and the Lord on High (*Shang Di*) and Ricci certainly sought to argue that traditional Chinese ritual practices, such as ancestor worship, were perfectly compatible with Christian faith. But in the bitter disputes between different Christian groups on that issue (the so-called Rites Controversy) that view was defeated, and successive popes (Innocent X in 1645, Benedict XIV in 1742) issued edicts that those practices were to be forbidden to Chinese converts to Christianity. The response of the Kangxi Emperor and his successors was eventually to ban the Jesuits and then to expel them.

But long before the arrival of those Jesuits in the sixteenth century, the Chinese had a rich literature in which they were the ones who controlled the terms of the comparison. They were surrounded by non-Han peoples whom they considered barbarians, though this was not because their languages were unintelligible (the Greek 'barbarian' comes from their perception that those who spoke other languages just made noises: 'bar-bar'). So it is worth considering how comparison worked out when it was the Chinese in control.

Unlike the Greeks, the Chinese had no awe-inspiring models of powerful states on their borders, even though their history is punctuated by recurrent conquests by foreigners: Tibetans, Uighurs, Jürchens, Mongols, Manchus. Yet the eventual adoption, by most of those foreigners, of Chinese ways could be cited as proof of Chinese superiority in civilisation even if not sometimes in military might. But Chinese ambivalence towards non-Han peoples is betrayed in the first instance by the names they gave to the groups they knew, for in many cases those names incorporated the radicals of animals, the dog especially.[3] That does not mean that the Chinese saw them *as* dogs. It is true that a number of weird and wonderful monstrous creatures are described in such texts as the *Shanhaijing*:[4] winged creatures, creatures like humans but with no heads, or with ears down to their knees, where it is not at all clear what either the authors or their readers believed, though the authors no doubt thought they would impress by their claimed knowledge of exotica from faraway places (just as Herodotus or Strabo or Pliny or Solinus did in the Greco-Roman world).

But as regards the peoples the Chinese actually dealt with in their own territories and on their borders (as opposed to those they just fantasised about beyond them), they were strange, no doubt, but human beings all the same. The Chinese term *ren*, like the Greek *anthrōpos*, covers humans in general, male and female, non-Han as well as Han. A notable text in the third century BCE compilation, the *Lüshi chunqiu* (19/6/2), says so explicitly with regard to two minority peoples, the Man and the Yi:

> Despite their backward tongues, their different customs and odd practices, despite their clothes, caps and belts, houses and encampments, boats, carts, vessels and tools, and despite their preferences of sound, sight and flavour all being different from ours, [they] are one with us and the same as us in satisfying their desires.

Comparing, as we saw, and as this text exemplifies, can be a way of asserting superiority by remarking that the others are both like us and yet unlike us. Those others have boats, but they are different from ours – and, no doubt the thought was, not as good as ours. They have customs, but that too marks them as inferior – 'odd' – as does the fact that they enjoy different foods and drinks and so on.

But the text also shows how comparison can be used, just as much, to identify a commonality. We all have the same basic needs, the same feelings

---

[3] I discussed this in Lloyd (2004: ch. 11).

[4] The *Shanhaijing* is another composite work with strata nowadays very variously dated, mostly between the fourth century BCE and the second century CE. See Fracasso (1993).

and desires.[5] Indeed the text goes on to say that in those respects even sage kings and legendary tyrants are on a par, even though the former were positive ideals of behaviour, the latter negative ones. So while comparison can underline and even celebrate difference, it can equally well proclaim unity. But in either case we can see that in the logic of the situation, emphasising the one means de-emphasising the other.

Which way a particular society, or a particular group within a society, will go, whether towards the 'we are special' pole, or to the 'we are all the same' one, will depend on all sorts of factors which certainly defy generalisation – nor shall I attempt one here. These may range from aspirations to political or military hegemony, or to being the one people chosen by God, through a sense of the need to close ranks in the face of threats from outsiders, real or imaginary, all the way to reflections on perceived biological, social, moral or even religious commonalities. Which pole one veers towards evidently has fundamental ethical consequences. Stepping outside one's own group, to consider alternatives to what it insists makes it the group it is, is always going to be difficult and will often be met with punitive sanctions. However, we should not suppose that scepticism and criticism of received ideas only exist in literate societies, since there is plenty of evidence that they are to be found also in non-literate ones.[6]

Thus far we have seen some examples of three of the valences of comparatism that I identified at the outset: to claim superiority, to register others' superiority and to recognise commonalities. In each case the assumption is that the other is intelligible. But I must now turn to those cases where that is doubted or denied. Often, to be sure, the others in view are not thought to pose problems, as when they are swiftly cast in the role of the seriously defective – a move that effectively disenfranchises them from the debate. But reflection on their difference may lead to bafflement and incomprehensibility.

When incomprehensibilities threaten, when we are faced not just with the problem of understanding others, but of the very possibility of human understanding as a whole, the reaction in different areas of experience

---

[5] The idea that all humans are linked by the desires we all experience can also be found in Greco-Roman sources, of course. Theophrastus, the source for Porphyry *On Abstinence* 2.32.3, even extended the commonality to other animals, a possible antecedent to the Stoic doctrine of *oikeiōsis* (affinity), though Chrysippus excluded animals. Cicero reports the Stoic view that mutual attraction between humans is natural, so that the mere fact that someone is a human makes it incumbent on another human not to treat him as alien (*On Ends* 3 62). Ancient Greek and other ideas of the relations between humans and other animals are discussed in Sorabji (1993), Osborne (2007), Lloyd (2012a: ch. 1).

[6] The notion that literacy favoured the development of criticism and scepticism was a key argument in Goody (1977), about which I have expressed my reservations in Lloyd (2014).

may be quite diverse. Scientists are as aware as anyone of the limits of what is currently understood, but even in the face of seemingly intractable problems there is generally a streak of optimism. Surely in the future someone will be able to crack the problem, where at present there is just aporia: surely some day the Grand Unified Theory will be secured. Yet it can be argued that as the frontiers of science expand, so too does the sense of what is beyond those frontiers, maybe at an even faster rate than that of the advances in understanding.

In the face of what is not yet known, science likes to assume it may one day have the answer. The response of religions of all kinds is very different,[7] for they often seek to emphasise, even to glorify, rather than to minimise, the mysterious, the ineffable, what is beyond mere mortal comprehension. When human words fail, maybe we shall be being encouraged to acts of reverence, or submission, or at least of humility. Rather than attempt to expand our understanding we may be told to abandon any such ambition. Reason and inquiry are no use. What is needed is faith. But to those who might then question, 'faith in what?' the reaction has generally been to anathematise any such doubters. Wherever the institutions of the religion are powerful enough, the authorities are likely to impose, as we said, the direst sanctions. Once again issues of control are at stake.

But we should observe how, even in that last case, comparatism is at work. When human knowers do not succeed, then we may be told we need a divine one who will, and in the process God's omniscience has to be modelled on, even while it must be contrasted with, fallible mortal understanding. The theological *via negativa* depends at every point on comparison. God's power and knowledge are not like ours, but again *are* true power and knowledge, fulfilling the criteria for such vastly more amply than anything we are capable of. God's being everywhere is modelled on our being somewhere, though God is nowhere in particular. Even the ineffable may always be *said to be* ineffable.

Doubts may well be expressed by the insider about how far any outsider is able to comprehend what is being said or to grasp the meaning of ritual acts. Most faiths will at some stage demand a certain suspension of disbelief. When, as often, what is offered as the truth about reality or the

---

[7] It should not be thought that I am here endorsing a facile dichotomy between the so-called Two Cultures, science and the humanities. In particular I would insist on certain shared cognitive and epistemological principles at work across that supposed divide. We can never bracket out the knowing subject from the known object, despite the fashion for an utterly impersonal style in scientific publications. Conversely, the humanities ignore what science has to tell us only at the cost of their own impoverishment.

divine or the human condition consists in a set of suggestive analogies, models or images, these will always be liable to multiple interpretations.[8] But at points paradox and obscurity may – we may suspect – be being deliberately cultivated precisely in order to establish a distance between believer and non-believer.

But obviously many of the problems where we are faced with the apparently incomprehensible do not stem from any deliberate mystification. We have no need to suspect that in the radically divergent ontological regimes that are reported by the anthropologists and that I introduced in Chapter 1. Let me now bring to bear my taxonomy of the valences of comparatism to see what light they can throw on the interpretative options open to us on these disputed issues.

Of course in the early days of the emergence of the discipline of anthropology the beliefs and practices reported from the field were regularly labelled 'primitive' to contrast them with those of the members of 'civilised' societies who were doing the reporting. 'Their' naïve and superstitious ideas often served as a foil, bolstering a sense of the superiority of more advanced societies, whose progress could be gauged by using that very contrast. Those primitive societies were held to offer some kind of window on the past of the human race, even though their members lived in the here and now. In Descola's schema it is still the case that 'naturalism', as he calls it, generally assumes its own correctness and would claim to be able to diagnose and avoid the errors of 'animism', 'totemism' and 'analogism'.

At the opposite end of the spectrum, however, there are (as I noted) those who hold not just that different ontological regimes diverge, but that they are strictly mutually unintelligible.[9] The stunning divergences

---

[8] To give an idea of the comprehensiveness of the system of analogies sometimes constructed in the context of religious belief and practice, let me quote an Indian example, an extensive passage from the opening of the *Bṛhadāraṇyaka Upaniṣad* relating the parts of a sacrificial horse to the universe. 'The head of the sacrificial horse, clearly, is the dawn – its sight is the sun; its breath is the wind; and its gaping mouth is the fire common to all men. The body of the sacrificial horse is the year – its back is the sky; its abdomen is the intermediate region; its underbelly is the earth; its flanks are the quarters; its ribs are the intermediate quarters; its limbs are the seasons; its joints are the months and fortnights; its feet are the days and nights; its bones are the stars; its flesh is the clouds; its stomach contents are the sand; its intestines are the rivers; its liver and lungs are the hills; its body hairs are the plants and trees; its forequarter is the rising sun; and its hindquarter is the setting sun. When it yawns, lightning flashes; when it shakes itself, it thunders; and when it urinates, it rains. Its neighing is speech itself' (Olivelle 1996: 7). The *Upaniṣads* set out extensive debates between rival gurus on the most abstruse questions. These characteristically end with the victory of one guru and the humiliation of his opponents, but the basis on which that victory has been gained is usually quite unclear: cf. Lloyd (2014: ch. 1).

[9] This was the subject of a heated debate on 'understanding a primitive society' in the late 50s, 60s and 70s, in which the key players included Winch (1958, 1964), MacIntyre (1967), Horton (1967), Lukes (1967), Gellner (1973), Barnes (1973) and Skorupski (1976).

in fundamental ideas about what there is that have been identified in the ethnography certainly give us pause. Yet a balance needs to be struck. We can see that very different notions of personhood, agency, space, animals, the human and the divine, are entertained and correspond to very different lived experiences, with very different attitudes to the basic human relations of giving, exchanging, producing, protecting, and the other practices that provide the framework for Descola's discussions (cf. p. 18). But the very fact that these differences can be compared, as differences in the idea of what counts as a person, for example, shows, or at least suggests to me as an outsider, that some beginnings of understanding are possible. That in turn implies that we can learn, as of course the anthropologists who do the fieldwork learn,[10] even if most of us, who are mere spectators, find it so much more difficult to do so.

So the examination of the divergences between ontologies need not, indeed should not, be carried out with the aim of deciding which is the unique 'correct' view, as if we could attach the labels true or false to each one taken as a whole. Judging between them does not involve a transcendent meta-language – as I said in Chapter 1, there is no such thing – but just a readiness to question the usual assumptions about fundamental categories that are made in our, or any given, language. Other natural languages may or may not have categories that correspond, however approximately, to ours – whether on the question of the person, or on causation, on God, on religion or on mythology – or, in my view, on 'nature' itself. But then it is a question of attending scrupulously to *what* categories the actors themselves use and of seeing where they do or do not correspond to whatever we initially bring to the discussion, and in the latter case especially being prepared to adjust those original ideas accordingly. And again as I said before (pp. 19–20), we should allow that the actors we are dealing with are themselves engaged in a similar anthropological exercise of attempting to match their ideas to those that they encounter.

We should be careful not to represent what it is to understand an ontology on the model of our grasping communications about mundane facts of everyday life. Cosmologies are not generally encapsulated in well-formed formulae and normally allow a good deal of room for interpretive

---

[10] What they claim to have come to understand differs, of course, and is often disputed, as is also the case with whatever they go on to accept on their own account. But access to the Other in anthropology, in history, and in many other aspects of experience, brings with it those opportunities, to increase understanding and to revise our initial assumptions, whether or not we are successful in doing so.

manoeuvre.[11] Even when we are faced with more explicit, potentially con-
flicting, ontological statements, our reaction should be to explore what
lessons they may have for us, particularly with regard to their implications
for our understanding of our relations with other human beings and even
with non-human animals. That does not mean that in the final analysis we
attempt to agree in some way with every view and practice we encounter.
There are good moral grounds for rejecting the views of those who would
limit what is a human being to their own group and who then feel free
to treat outsiders in any way they like. In that remark I presuppose that
morality too can be discussed fruitfully across cultures, though that is not
to commit to some rigid set of universal rules.

When we start piecing together commonalities, we are likely to begin
with our shared human biology. We have seen that some such recognition
is not limited to Western modernity but can be found in ancient Greece
and ancient China – and no doubt in many other societies as well. Yet
biology is clearly not what a great many other cultures would focus on.
Nor is it unproblematic for us. While some would emphasise what marks
out humans from other animals (without necessarily going as far as to say,
with Genesis, that we were given dominion over them), others would insist
on what we have in common with other creatures. We may not have a
myth about their origins and ours; but we have an evolutionary story, for
sure, both a purely biological one and one that attempts an account of the
gradual cultural evolution of humans compared with other animals (cf. e.g.
Tooby and Cosmides 1992).

So when we turn to what we all too often unguardedly take to be the
antonym of 'nature', namely 'culture', the situation is more complex still,
even before we take into account the rich variety of human social arrange-
ments reported in ethnography. On the one hand, we can recognise certain
commonalities here too. As the 'political' animals we are (in Aristotle's
terms), we all have *some* social and cultural engagements, though of course
not the same ones. To begin with, every human society is faced with the
question of who is to be allowed to marry whom: every society has to deal
with its dead. The problems are constants, even though the solutions differ
so widely.

On the other hand, taking a leaf out of the ethologists' book, we can see
that we do not need to refer to the other ontological regimes reported by
anthropologists in order to accept that 'culture' and 'social relations' should

[11] That is of course not to deny that within any cosmology commitments to what is straightforwardly
the case may be made and may be judged to be correct or mistaken. I shall exemplify this in
Chapter 5.

not be denied to other animals – so 'ours' (whatever they are) should be judged by criteria that include 'theirs'. All humans use languages, but again it is only if we wished to restrict language to verbalisation that we would want entirely to deny language to other animals, and that restriction does not tally with our sense of our own human non-verbal communications.

In those remarks I have put comparatism to work, comparing humans and other animals and comparing divergent ontological regimes. I started by observing how comparatism has often been used to claim superiority, to impose control, to exclude outsiders, to throttle criticism or dissent. As a tool for organising phenomena it can have devastating negative effects. But it clearly need not be used to exclude: it need not imply a privileged vantage point from which to look down on everyone else. It may even be a stimulus to revision, to criticism and to dissent – which is where my fifth valence comes into its own, allowing for differences but not in a bid to determine hierarchies of superiority or inferiority, nor yet to proclaim mutual unintelligibilities, but rather to make the most of the opportunities for broadening our horizons that those differences present.

Its most ambitious use, to compare ways of being in the world and even ontological regimes themselves, can yield important insights, provided certain conditions are met. On the one hand, as I said, the aim should not be some justification of just the one regime, some version of naturalism perhaps with which we may begin, though that has often been the effect of many restrictive views (and not just Western ones) about the truly human. On the other, we should not suppose that insurmountable barriers of mutual unintelligibility rule out any possibility of progress in understanding even the radically Other. For this we need, among other things, to be prepared to suspend many of our pet assumptions, including even the naturalness of the nature/culture dichotomy. But that in turn does not mean renouncing the possibility of any critical judgement, as if we could agree with whatever seems to be implied by any given regime, for there are, as we said, ethical as well as scientific questions on which we have to take a stand. Rather, the first positive lesson we can take away is again to do with pluralism or as I call it the multidimensionality of the phenomena: to put it at its most banal, it is important not to reduce what it is to be a human being to a single dimension, while we recognise that we have much still to learn about the multidimensionality in question. And the second, linguistic counterpart of that is to allow for semantic stretch. The striving for univocity and a *per genus et differentiam* definition of 'human' are both ways that are liable to lead to the denial of that multidimensionality.

Recognition of different natural languages has often been used covertly to downgrade everyone else's in relation to your own mother tongue (the one, indeed, you claim to be truly 'natural'). But the fact that all humans use complex languages can be cited as one commonality between us. For sure, that does not take us very far, but it is a fact nevertheless and it has important implications for our investigations of analogies. Since every language has to proceed by way of general terms that imply explicit or implicit appeals to similarities and differences, that provides (as I have mentioned before) a strong argument for the inevitable use of comparisons of some sort. That of course leaves open the questions of which comparisons those will be, and whether they are well grounded, and again of who is in a position to pronounce on that issue. A crucial problem to which I shall be returning in later chapters relates to the extent to which comparing as a whole, whether of the explicit or the implicit variety, is open to challenge, which in turn takes us to the issue of how far attempts are, or should be, made to downgrade or undermine comparisons that do not meet strict conditions laid down in a bid to ensure their validity.

As with any other tool, there are good and bad ways of using comparison – and if the argument I have just mounted is accepted, to the effect that some use of this particular tool is inevitable, then that makes understanding its different valences so much more important. Unmasking how it has been abused at different junctures, for different purposes and with different covering justifications, by those with authority and power and by those without, is an important task. But when all the unmasking, the demythologising, the demystifying, have been done, we face the substantive problems I have been discussing of what we should say about commonalities and about diversities, in relation to the humanity of human beings in the first instance, but in every subject where we are trying to push back the frontiers of knowledge. For that, open-minded, even-handed, comparatism of the type I have endeavoured to exemplify is essential.

If we want to understand what it is to be a human being, what it is to be good, what it is to know, what we can hope for (to transpose Kant's programme) then we need all the resources of history, of biology, of evolutionary psychology, of social anthropology, of philosophy, even to begin to sketch an answer, well aware that what we might antecedently anticipate the answers to be will be a tangled web stemming from our own formation, our environment and the narratives we have always been busy constructing of our *raisons d'être*. So if all our starting assumptions must be treated as revisable, we can nevertheless learn to revise them, in particular by pondering the lessons to be gathered from the radically Other. So far from being a means of dismissing and downgrading ideas and practices that differ from our own, comparatism can be a key resource for that project of self-criticism and revision. In the next chapter my main task will be to probe the use of analogies in discussions of ethical issues in particular, where, as we shall see, attempts, sometimes misguided ones, have been made to provide safeguards against their fallibility and deceptiveness.

CHAPTER 3

Analogies, images and models in ethics: some first-order and second-order observations on their use and evaluation in ancient Greece and China

The primary aim of this chapter is to investigate the use of analogies, images and models in ethical discourse, their modalities and their justification. How far can they, or should they, be replaced by arguments that do not suffer from the shortcomings of analogies? I shall concentrate on two of the richest sources of analogical reasoning in ethics, from the two ancient societies that are the usual focus of my investigation, Greece and China. How are analogies used, which types are privileged, and how were they evaluated by those who employed them or who criticised their use? For that last purpose we shall need to consider more broadly the ideals of reasoning that were proposed. Greece and China evidently represent only a small section of the possible subject-matter, but they offer opportunities to assess different approaches and ambitions, and they enable, in particular, some typical Western preoccupations to be placed in perspective, thereby contributing to my strategic aim in these studies.

Arguably, in ethics, as in most other fields of inquiry, analogies, models and images provide one of the commonest modes of argument to recommend a point of view. No one will deny that they are extremely pervasive, both as explicit comparisons and as implicit ones. The latter are usually labelled metaphors – as in Lakoff and Johnson's classic study (1980) *The Metaphors We Live By* – although I have expressed my reservations about the use of that term, not least as it tends to be employed to downgrade a certain kind of language use by contrast with a 'literal' or 'strict' acceptance.

But if my general point about pervasiveness is accepted, there is nothing surprising in the fact that analogies and images are so common in early Chinese and Greco-Roman ethics in particular. The interesting questions relate not to the fact that there are lots of comparisons of different types, but rather to which ones were favoured (my first-order question), and secondly, and more importantly, to how they were deployed, for example how self-consciously and how critically (my second-order one).

If we ask the first, simpler, question of which analogies, models and images are privileged, I have first to say that to review these at all thoroughly would require a monograph or two, so I must be highly selective. We may make a start by referring to some of the recurrent cosmological images found, for each of the main types carries ethical and more particularly political implications. At first glance at least, the similarities between two of the main groups of such images in China and in the Greco-Roman world are very striking. Both ancient civilisations often picture the cosmos as a state, both often also do so as a living being (the third common Greco-Roman image of the cosmos as an artefact is less often found in China). The kind of state used as a model, monarchic, oligarchic, democratic, even anarchic, differs as between different Greek and Roman writers, while the Chinese generally think in terms of the monarchic political system that was always their ideal. But whatever human model is adopted, there are clear implications for the relationship, within the state, between rulers and ruled. In particular, as in the very common Chinese motif, each should know their place.[1] Similarly when the cosmos is conceived as a living organism, the proper functioning of its components likewise carries potential lessons for cooperative endeavour.

But even if we stay at that rather elevated level of generalisation, certain differences also emerge, over and above the diversity of Greek political imagery that I have already mentioned. One important point may be expressed like this. Although we may loosely think of the Chinese images as microcosm–macrocosm analogies, more strictly they are not analogies between terms that are by implication clearly separated as belonging to different domains, but rather all examples of the same patterns, in the heavens, in humans and in the state. Analogies, the point is, implicitly, and often explicitly, recognise differences between the comparanda. The heavens, humans and the state, for the Chinese, tend to form a seamless whole, though of course that does not mean that the Chinese failed to distinguish them at all. The *Dao*, and the interactions of yin and yang, are at work everywhere, but that is not to ignore that there are different manifestations of this in different contexts.

---

[1] This is a common theme in the *Lunyu* which used to be ascribed to Confucius himself (whose traditional dates are 551–479 BCE) though it is now generally agreed to be a composite work put together by his disciples in the 250 years or so after his death. Thus at 13.3, when Confucius is asked what he would give priority to, if the Lord of Wei asked him to run the government, he is represented as replying 'rectify names'. But this turns out to be less a matter of semantics than of morality and social order. The concern is less with words corresponding to things, than of things – specifically social ranks – corresponding to their proper names (those laid down by the sage kings). The theme recurs repeatedly in later writers, starting with *Xunzi* 22 in the third century BCE.

True, we should recognise that some Greco-Roman cosmological images also elide or minimise the differences between the comparanda. While the cosmos is sometimes viewed as *like* a state or *like* a living organism, it is also sometimes said to *be* a state or to be alive (cf. Lloyd 1966: 416). From the point of view of ethical messages, however, the key issue is that we are all in it together, all components of a political entity, all members indeed of the body politic. Good behaviour, in both ancient civilisations, is often construed as contributing to the health of that body politic, deviant behaviour is pathological: a disease in fact that has to be treated, in other words punished.[2] While notions of health and disease differ widely, between Chinese and Greek writers, and also *within* both Chinese and Greek medicine, the common thought is that the well-being of the political state is modelled on the health of the physical individual. The statesman is the doctor of the body politic and can diagnose and cure its ills even when they are not recognised as such by ordinary lay folk or idiots. In the *Lüshi chunqiu* (20/5/1) the text diagnoses blockages in the human body, in nature (trees and plants) and in the state as the cause of problems: in the last case the ruler's power does not circulate freely and the people's desires are frustrated. The solution is that sage rulers should trust their worthy advisers, including of course the person who was responsible for compiling this text! This was Lü Buwei, who was chief minister to the king of Qin, who was later to unite the empire as Qin Shi Huang Di.

Among the many other images that are pressed into service with similar messages, one particularly prominent one is that of harmony, the harmonious, the concordant. Here too there are possible divergences, since the emphasis may be, but is not necessarily, on the difference between the elements that are or should be brought into harmony.[3] Just as a musical harmony is between higher and lower notes, so a political one is between superiors and inferiors. The additional point here is that musical harmony is not just a model for good relations within the state: music, in both Greece and China, is an essential part of the education of the good person, the good citizen, the *junzi*. And that is true of some music very much more than of other kinds. Writers in both ancient cultures are emphatic about the disastrous effects of listening to licentious music, where again you will need guidance from teachers who can indeed distinguish the good modes

---

[2] I collected a good deal of evidence for this point in ancient Greece in Lloyd (2003).
[3] Horden and Hsu (2013) collect interesting discussions of the varying notions of balance and harmony to be found in different ancient, medieval and modern medical traditions.

from the bad ones. Confucius will tell you about this in China,[4] and Plato goes on about the subject at length in the *Republic* and the *Laws*.

In the instances I have so far mentioned, there are close resemblances, as well as certain differences, between the analogies, models and images we find in our two ancient civilisations. But other groups of images exhibit more profound contrasts. Take those that surround notions of stability and of interdependence. Many Greeks had a horror of stasis, political revolution or faction, to the point where any political change was viewed with some suspicion, although that attitude should be set against the background of the frequent actual political revolutions that many Greek states experienced (cf. Loraux 2002 [1987]).

The Chinese, on the other hand, knew that no dynasty would last for ever. It is true that the first Emperor, Qin Shi Huang Di, whom I have just mentioned, imagined that the one he founded would keep going for ten thousand generations. But he is something of an exception to the general rule of the Chinese recognition of the permanence of change. Although Chinese tables of opposites look, on the face of it, very much like Greek ones (as indeed I argued in Lloyd 1966), that masks a more fundamental difference (as I eventually pointed out in Lloyd 1996a). Where for some Greeks the ideal was that of the independence of the items in one column from those in the other, the Chinese more readily acknowledged, indeed insisted upon, their interdependence. That applies particularly to the key contrast between yin and yang, for even when yang is at its height, there are traces of emerging yin, and vice versa. Of course the Greeks appreciated that male and female need to copulate to reproduce, while they still fantasised about autochthony, birth from the earth, without females (while in China there are commoner stories about births from females alone, parthenogenesis: they too can be found in the West, of course).[5] Again Greeks were aware that masters needed slaves, and yet the ideal there too was one of the independence of the superior from the inferior. Once again, however, there are exceptions, for while the Pythagorean *sustoichia* (Table of Opposites) stressed opposition, Heraclitus certainly asserted the

---

[4] In the *Lunyu* (15.11) when asked about how to govern a state, Confucius specifies the calendar to be adopted, the type of carriage to be used and even the cap to be worn, and then goes on: 'for music adopt the *shao* and *wu* [that is the music of the sage kings Shun and Wu]. Get rid of the sounds of Zheng [a southern state] and banish clever talkers. The sounds of Zheng are licentious and clever talkers are a menace.' Conversely, when Confucius was in the state of Qi and heard the *shao*, he did not notice the taste of meat for three months (*Lunyu* 7.14).

[5] In the *Shiji* (the first major universal history, composed around 100 BCE) the beginning of both the Yin and the Zhou dynasties is marked by a woman becoming pregnant without copulating with a male (*Shiji* 3: 91.1ff.; 4: 111.1ff.).

interdependence of opposites of every kind, including good and evil. Once again he defeats efforts to generalise about *the* Greek attitude to opposites.

It is obvious enough, we may say, that the political and ethical analogies, models and images for which we have evidence in China or in Greece provide us with plenty of opportunities to explore the deep-seated assumptions made not just about good and evil, but also about humans, about the similarities and differences between humans and other animals, about agency, and about causation. Their images and models are certainly good for us to think with, when we address such questions ourselves. At the same time we have to recognise that most of the generalisations that we might propose, both about similarities between those two ancient civilisations, and about differences, are subject to exceptions and reservations. Neither ancient society was without its disagreements, disputes or controversies, on ethical matters as on the understanding of the physical world. Those disputes may be particularly violent in ancient Greece: but there are plenty of hard-hitting ones also in China as I shall be illustrating immediately.

My next question is trickier, for it concerns just how analogies, models and images were used in ethics, how self-consciously and how critically. What assumptions did ancient writers themselves make about their use? We move from our, observers', judgements to their actors' ones. The famous controversy over human *xing* (our innate characteristics) between Mencius, Gaozi and Xunzi illustrates two fundamental points: first, how the argument proceeds almost exclusively via analogy and counter-analogy, and, secondly, the implicit recognition that those analogies are not conclusive. Gaozi, as reported by Mencius at least in the fourth century BCE, argued that human nature is indifferent, neither good nor bad. It is like willow wood that can be made into different objects: cups and bowls for instance. Mencius' comment was that that depended on human intervention, the person doing the carving or cutting.

But Gaozi has a second analogy: that of a whirlpool. 'If you open a channel for it in the East, it will flow to the East, but if you open a channel in the West, it flows westward. Man's nature has neither good nor bad allotted to it, just as water has neither East nor West allotted to it' (*Mencius* 6A/1, 6A/2). But Mencius counters that one by pointing out that water does have a tendency to flow downwards. Similarly, according to Mencius, human nature has a tendency to be good, a point in support of which he invokes how anyone who sees a child about to fall down a well spontaneously goes to the rescue (*Mencius* 2A/6). That is an argument from example, of course, rather than by analogy, but that still depends on a recognition that the example is a typical one, to reveal a basic feature of human nature – which raises the question of its relationship with other examples. We are back to the problem of recognising similarities across species or across genera.

It is not just the water image that is used in two contrasting ways. When Xunzi in the third century returns to the controversy, he appropriates the wood analogy to argue for a very different thesis from either Gaozi's or Mencius', namely that human nature is evil – a proposition that entails interesting complications in relation to what Xunzi has to say about human educability. Humans, he held, are naturally evil, though they have a potentiality to be good, an essential addition, of course, if Xunzi is to justify his claim to be able to teach virtue. Now humans are compared to crooked wood, which has to be forced straight. 'Crooked wood inevitably requires steaming and straightening with the arrow-straightener to straighten it... and granted that human nature is bad, it inevitably requires teachers and standards to correct it' (*Xunzi* 23: 5ff.).[6]

This stunning sequence of analogies shows pretty clearly that they are understood to be inconclusive. Everything depended on the acceptance of the positive analogy. Given that the two comparanda are never identical, the negative analogy or points of difference between the two must be discounted. There are plenty of similar examples in Greek ethical discourse. Take the suggestion that the ruler is like a shepherd to his flock. One side argued that this shows that the ruler should care for his subjects, but that was countered by the observation that the shepherd does not tend his sheep for their sake, but rather out of his own interests (in Plato's *Republic* 343b Thrasymachus takes the latter view, while Socrates argues for the former at 345cd).

Yet it is one thing for an interlocutor not to accept a particular analogy in a particular context: it is another to question analogical reasoning as such. Chinese writers, as we have seen, contest particular analogies often enough, but how far do they proceed to a general critique of analogising as a whole? The answer brings to light further interesting similarities and differences between China and Greece.

Let me turn first to the different levels of explicit objection that we find in Greek writers. A well-known passage in the *Gorgias* (490e–491a) shows how an objector may protest not just about a single analogy, but a whole collection of them. Callicles there says that Socrates is always going on about cobblers and fullers and cooks and doctors who have nothing to do with the subject in hand – at least that is what Callicles claims. But

---

[6] The image of needing to straighten warped wood recurs in Aristotle's *Nicomachean Ethics* 1109b5–7.

then there are also texts that go a stage further and point out how images and resemblances in general are (or may be) misleading. Again Plato is a rich source. Images, *eikones*, come in for a lot of criticism when they are contrasted with proofs, *apodeixeis*. When in one of the discussions of the soul's immortality Simmias offers an *eikōn*, namely that the soul may be an attunement, he goes on to concede that he has given no more than a likely and specious argument. 'I am well aware that theories that base their proofs on what is plausible are imposters: unless one is on one's guard, they deceive one very badly, in geometry and everything else' (*Phaedo* 92cd).

Again in both the *Phaedrus* (262a–c) and the *Sophist* (231a) the deceptiveness of likenesses is exposed. In the former text it is recognised that similarities may be deliberately used to deceive, proceeding little by little by means of likenesses from what is to its opposite. In the latter dialogue when Theaetetus thinks they have found 'what looks like' the sophist, the Eleatic Stranger remarks: 'so too a wolf looks like a dog, the one a most fierce, the other a most tame animal. But a careful person should always be on his guard against resemblances above all, for they are a most slippery tribe', thereby, by a nice irony, using first an analogy and then an image to make the point that resemblances may be deceptive.

Aristotle in turn goes much further in his condemnation, in certain contexts at least, of what he now explicitly labels *metaphora*, where the root meaning is 'transfer'. They should not be used in definitions, we are told at *Posterior Analytics* 97b37–9, and of course Aristotle shares with Socrates and with Plato the idea of the cardinal importance, especially in ethics, of defining your terms. Criticising Empedocles' notion that the sea is the sweat of the earth, Aristotle says (*Meteorologica* 357a24–6) that that may be adequate for the purposes of poetry, for *metaphora* is poetical – but it is not adequate for understanding the nature [of the thing]. Again, notoriously, when launching one of his attacks against Plato's theory of Forms (*Metaphysics* 991a20–2, 1079b24–6), Aristotle puts it that 'to say that they [the Forms] are models and that other things share in them is to speak nonsense and to use poetic metaphors'.

Yet when he deals with poetics and rhetoric themselves we realise that not all Aristotle's assessments of *metaphora* are negative, though this point generally receives less attention in the modern secondary literature. They have an important contribution to make to the excellence of style.[7] Skill in their use, he says in the *Poetics* 1459a6–8, is indeed a mark of natural ability

---

[7] Comparison or similarity, *bi*, is used to define one particular type of poetry in China, see Cheng (1979), though it would be a mistake to think that similarities and images are confined to that type.

(*euphuia*), explaining that with the remark that to use *metaphora* well is to observe likeness. In the *Rhetoric* too, 1405a8–10, 1410b33–4, the correct use of *metaphora* produces perspicacity, pleasure and a foreign air, and is not something that can be learnt from anyone else. Metaphors bring matters 'before the eyes' (*pro ommatōn*) and make descriptions vivid, lively, witty.

But are metaphors merely good for stylistic effect? We find Aristotle himself using lots of transferred expressions in his own discussions of rhetoric, but are they to be confined to that domain? It is above all in connection with his notion of demonstration that metaphors are condemned. Where Plato never specified what counted for him as proper proofs, Aristotle certainly did, laying down, in the *Posterior Analytics*, the conditions that had to be met to produce the strictest mode of demonstration. While he recognises looser forms of demonstrating, including what he calls 'rhetorical' ones, *rhētorikai apodeixeis*, nevertheless, for natural science and for metaphysics, only strict demonstrations will do and they depend first on the ultimate primary premises being self-evidently true, and, secondly, on the demonstration proceeding by way of valid deductive arguments. But those arguments, he thought, had to be syllogistic, and that in turn meant that the univocity of the terms used was essential. Any departure from strict univocity would destroy the transitivity of entailment. So while metaphor has its place in poetry and in rhetoric, it is excluded from any inquiry that aimed at the highest form of demonstration.

But what about ethics in particular? Aristotle makes some important concessions concerning the degree of exactness to be expected in ethics: it is as inappropriate to demand demonstration in ethics as it is to allow a mathematician to use merely probable arguments (*Nicomachean Ethics* 1094b12–13, 25–7). So ethics is recognised to deal with truths that hold not just always, but also for the most part,[8] and it has to do with terms that are applied *kath' homoiotēta*, that is in virtue of a similarity. Someone who is fearless in the face of poverty or disease is not truly courageous, Aristotle says, though that term is applied to such persons thanks to a similarity with the real virtue (*Nicomachean Ethics* 1115a19). Similarly at 1134a28–30, when he limits political justice to those who are free and equal, he concedes that justice 'of a sort' and 'by way of similarity' exists elsewhere too, and at 1138b5–6 'by way of similarity' is paired with 'metaphorically'. Yet these derived usages all pick out cases that fall short of the true virtues

---

[8] Yet in the *Posterior Analytics* Aristotle attempts to include in his discussion of proof syllogisms where the propositions are true only 'for the most part', though his efforts are hardly successful. Indeed they fail entirely if 'for the most part' is interpreted purely as a matter of frequency: see Mignucci (1981).

in question, which should in principle be given canonical definitions *per genus et differentiam*, as we say. Such definitions provide the ideal for any discourse, ethics included.

You need good judgement, practical wisdom, *phronēsis*, to get the right answers, and while that is classed as an intellectual excellence, it is crucially dependent on moral virtue. You cannot have the one without the other, for practical intelligence without moral virtue would be mere cunning, *deinotēs*, while moral virtue without *phronēsis* is no more than what he calls 'natural virtue', which children and even animals may share. I shall have more to say about the *phronimos* later, but for now may observe that the claims for ethics as a *technē* depend on its ability to give rational accounts of its subject-matter. From that point of view it has more in common with the ideals of the *Organon*, particularly with regard to the need for clarity in definition, than with rhetoric, when it focuses merely on persuasion, let alone with poetry.

Now one of the most striking differences between the ideals of reasoning that were developed in Greece and China relates to the development, in the former, of a notion of axiomatic-deductive proof, starting from self-evident, indemonstrable, primary premises and proceeding by deductive argument to incontrovertible conclusions. It is certainly far from the case that all Greek argument was set out in such a form or even aspired to such. But that was Aristotle's ideal and it was the chief pattern adopted in much (not all) of Greek mathematics from Euclid onwards. Yet, as I showed in Lloyd (1996a: ch. 3, 58–62), neither the notion nor the practice is found in Chinese writings until some time after the Jesuits used Euclid, or rather Clavius' Latin version of the first five books of the *Elements*, in their attempts to persuade the Chinese that such proofs are not just possible, but necessary, not just in mathematics, but in theology and elsewhere: and even then that Jesuit preoccupation did not cut much ice with many Chinese. Chinese mathematics, in particular, which is well represented in texts that date already from Han times,[9] never set its sights on delivering such, even though there is plenty of concern about checking that the results obtained are correct, including that the algorithms by which they were secured are sound (cf. below, Chapter 4). But that certainly does not mean that in China we find no general critical analyses of the use of images, resemblances and the like, in ethical matters and elsewhere. Two chapters in the *Lüshi chunqiu* are particularly interesting from the point of view

---

[9] Our main early Chinese mathematical text dates from the turn of the millennium. This is the *Jiuzhang suanshu* (*The Nine Chapters on Mathematical Procedures*), though we also possess an earlier shorter text, the *Suanshushu*, discovered in a tomb that was closed in 186 BCE.

of our comparison with the Greek criticisms I have just been discussing. But first let me cite a defence of the use of analogy mounted by Hui Shi, a philosopher and statesman of the third century BCE, famous for his paradoxes.

Our source is the *Shuo Yuan* (first-century BCE) which records a dialogue between Hui Shi and a king whom he served as minister. The king objects to Hui Shi's repeated use of analogies and demands direct speaking. Hui Shi replies (using an analogy indeed) that if someone did not know what a *dan* is (it is some kind of stringed instrument), it would be useless to say it is like a *dan*. But if the questioner is told it is like a bow but with a string made of bamboo, he will understand. So the king was quite wrong to try to prohibit analogies (*Shuo Yuan* 11.8, 87.22ff., cf. Graham 1989: 81).

In the *Lüshi chunqiu*, by contrast, the emphasis is rather on the possible deceptiveness of analogies. Book 22, ch. 3, is entitled 'spurious resemblances' (*yi si*). This starts off: 'what leads people to great confusion and error is assuredly the resemblances between objects'. Then we are given two examples from the crafts (not a million miles away, we might think, from Socrates): what bother jade cutters are stones that troublingly resemble, but are not, jade, while those who judge swords are bothered by swords that resemble the legendary blade from Gan (where those familiar with English legend might think of Excalibur) but are nothing like as good. What bothers worthy rulers next (the chief target of the whole discussion is a political one) is people who know a lot of things and whose skilled discourse makes them seem learned, when in fact they are not. 'The ruler of a doomed state may seem to be wise, the ministers of a doomed state may seem to be faithful. Resemblances between things greatly confuse the stupid, but cause the sage to reflect more deeply upon them.' 'It is essential', the chapter concludes, 'to examine thoroughly what lies behind spurious resemblances, and for that you need the right person.' The resemblances may not be called a 'slippery tribe', but the warnings concerning their deceptiveness could not be clearer. Moreover Plato's concern with unmasking those he calls sophists and pointing out that they are not philosophers is not too far away from the chief topic in the *Lüshi chunqiu* chapter, namely distinguishing wise from just seemingly wise advisers.

A second chapter, *bie lei*, 'different kinds', book 25, ch. 2, focuses on the importance of knowing precisely which objects belong together and which do not. This is a more general discussion, but again it comes to be applied in particular to ethics. It opens very Socratically: 'to know that one does not know is the loftiest of all [forms of awareness] . . . There are many things that, though they appear to be members of a particular kind, *lei*, are not . . . But when the kind to which a thing belongs is uncertain, what can be inferred about it?' There follow lots of examples, including simple mathematical and zoological ones (a small square and a large square belong to the same *lei*,[10] just as a small horse and a large one also do). But once again the text targets what one can say about species or kinds of morality and of understanding. You have to be able to distinguish good explanations from bad ones. 'This is what causes problems for loyal ministers and what causes the worthy to be dismissed' (25/2/3).

There is absolutely no question, then, that Chinese writers can and do move from first-order comments on particular analogies, models and images to second-order reflections on similarity and difference in general. There is just as much realisation of their possible deceptiveness as there is in Greek writers, and particular emphasis is placed, in those Chinese texts, on the relevance of that point to morality and politics, on the need for the sage ruler not to be taken in by misleading resemblances.

Thus far we may say that while both ancient societies make extensive use of analogies, models and images in ethics and elsewhere, the dangers of so doing are also pointed out. Yet there is no Chinese equivalent to the Greek ambition to construct a model of a style of reasoning that would be immune to those dangers, indeed to error of any kind – those Greek-style axiomatic-deductive demonstrations that would yield incontrovertible conclusions.

Those Greek notions and practices of proof have, of course, often been held up as triumphs of rationality, but to put the matter into proper perspective we have to recognise first that self-evident primary premises are far harder to come by in most disciplines (with the possible exception of mathematics) than many Greeks supposed, and, secondly and relatedly, that Greek attempts to apply that model in fields such as medicine or theology were decidedly misguided (cf. Lloyd 1996a: ch. 3 on Galen and Proclus). We come to the crux of the matter. We have seen that Aristotle is under no illusions that ethics is exact. Yet like Plato before him he hankered after proofs even in the fields of ethics and politics. In the highly competitive situation in Greek disputation, this was, in his view, the only sure way to guarantee results. Mere persuasions, even or especially the appeal to a majority vote, were certainly not enough to secure the truth or the right practical decision. While many of Aristotle's examples, in the *Posterior Analytics*, relate to mathematics, not all do, for quite a few come

[10] The first extant commentary on the *Jiuzhang suanshu*, by Liu Hui in the third century CE, pays much attention to the kinds, *lei*, into which mathematical shapes fall: see Chemla and Guo (2004: s.v. *lei*); cf. Lloyd (2009: 54).

from astronomy, meteorology or botany, not just eclipses, but broad-leaved deciduous trees, and, yes, even human affairs, the causes of the outbreak of war (94a36–b7). The mode of demonstration he so carefully constructs operates as an *ideal* far beyond mathematics, even though he is clearly not unaware of the difficulty of implementing it.

Now where analogies and images are concerned – where one might suppose there is no way in which they can be justified within the model – the tactic Aristotle uses, in his discussion of *paradeigma*, both in the *Organon* and in the *Rhetoric*, is to think of it as a two-stage argument. It proceeds neither from part to whole (induction) nor from whole to part (deduction) but from part to part. But when the universal can be secured by examination of similar cases, in the inductive move (his example at *Prior Analytics* 68b38–69a11 is again a moral one, the wrongness of waging war against neighbours), then the particular conclusion can thereafter be got deductively. So while normally paradigm uses incomplete induction, it is potentially justifiable if the induction is complete. That enables Aristotle to bring it, one might say, into the syllogistic fold, except that what is then justified is not analogy as such at all, but a combination of complete induction and deduction, where the stumbling block relates, of course, to the very possibility of a complete induction in the first place.[11]

So if we might admire Aristotle's bid to construct a schema of argument that will be immune to error, we have rather to admit that the Chinese were more realistic in never being distracted by any such ambition, in ethics in particular. Far more often they settled for suggestive analogies and indeed in many examples what precisely they were suggestive of is left open and different interlocutors will focus on different aspects of the parallelisms set up. They were aware, as we have seen, that analogies were inconclusive, and could be misleading, but they did not seek a formula that would *guarantee* their appropriateness. For that, what you needed was a sage ruler, for he could surely tell the difference between the appropriate and the deceptive resemblances. To the objection that that is not very helpful, because we cannot tell who *is* a sage ruler, the answer would be you have to work hard to learn who is, indeed to approximate to sagehood yourself, even if you

---

[11] In a similar move Aristotle brings some arguments from signs into good deductive order. His general term for signs is *sēmeion*, but he uses *tekmērion* for conclusive signs that can be converted into proper syllogisms (*Prior Analytics* II ch. 27 and *Rhetoric* I ch. 2). One of his examples of the latter (1357b14–17) is the inference that a woman has had a child from the fact that she has milk in her breasts (in the *Prior Analytics* he more unguardedly makes the inference to her being pregnant). An example of the former, a non-deductive inference, is the inference that a woman is pregnant from her sallow complexion (which may indicate pregnancy, but does not always do so). See especially Burnyeat (1982, 1994), Lloyd (2007b).

will never get there. At least on the way you avoid the trap of the belief that some purely abstract, logical, guarantee of success is available.

The final irony is that there is certainly one strand of Aristotle's thought in ethics that similarly puts the emphasis on the need for good judgement, namely his extensive discussion of *phronēsis* that I alluded to before. Like the Chinese sage ruler, the Aristotelian *phronimos* will get it right, thanks to his moral character as well as his practical intelligence (a theme much further developed, to be sure, in the Stoic ideal). From that perspective both Chinese and Greek thinkers show good sense, not least in a recognition of how difficult it is to get it right, to make the correct judgements in matters of morality. Yet if Aristotle was under no illusions in that regard, we have still to note how very un-Chinese he is in one respect, in his suggestion that the reasoning of the *phronimos* will be *syllogistic*, a matter of practical, not theoretical, syllogisms to be sure, but sharing with the theoretical the ideal of deductive rigour.[12] Experience is all very well, and may count for more, in practice, than being able to give a theoretical account:[13] and yet deductive rigour is still the ideal, an ambition that no Chinese sage would have dreamed of sharing.

But the question I must now press, finally, is what alternatives there are, short of Aristotelian axiomatic-deductive demonstration, that will help to secure conclusions in ethical reasoning. Of course Aristotle would insist that for strict demonstration the primary premises, if indeed they are primary, must be self-evident and indemonstrable, for if they can be demonstrated, they should be, and then they would not be primary premises. But that does not mean that there is no way in which we can assess the premises or assumptions we generally use in practical argumentation. Rather we can and do weigh them against alternatives, and that generally involves considering their consequences. When those consequences are seen to be unacceptable, the premises will need to be revised, as in *reductio* arguments and in the schema we call *modus tollens*. If A, then B. But not B. So not A.

Now while in ancient China there was no attempt to construct an ideal of axiomatic-deductive proof, there was, as I have noted already, plenty of concern with aspects of argument. That includes, notably, the need to

---

[12] The practical syllogism figures prominently in Aristotle's discussion of *akrasia* (weakness of will) and has attracted a lot of attention from commentators, especially those who share Aristotle's ambition to bring ethics within the scope of his analysis of formal logic.

[13] Thus in *Nicomachean Ethics* 1141b16–21 he remarks that a person who knows that 'light' meats are healthy but does not know which meats are 'light' is less able to secure health than someone who knows that chicken, for instance, is healthy but does not grasp why.

check for consistency, as in the famous and often cited case of the salesman who claimed that his lances could penetrate anything but also that his shields were able to withstand penetration from anything.[14] In his analysis of Chinese logic Harbsmeier (1998: 280–5) identified arguments that when formalised (and that point is important) correspond not just to *modus tollens*, but also to *modus ponens* (If A, then B. But A. So B), to arguments a fortiori and to what may loosely be called sorites arguments.[15]

But while, negatively, *reductio* is a powerful tool of criticism in any context, the more usual tactic to make a positive recommendation is, as we have seen, by way of example or analogy. Thus in the Mencius text, the view that human nature is good is supported by a striking example. We recognise that, when we see a child about to fall down a well, we all instinctively go to help it, not out of a desire to ingratiate ourselves with the child's parents, nor to avoid the discomfort the child's screams would cause us – but simply out of fellow-feeling. Mencius does not prove that all humans would, in fact, react in that way. He does not set up artificial situations in a psychological laboratory to test what different people's feelings might be. He just asserts that our shared humanity would dictate how we would behave.

But just as much as the more far-fetched comparisons with willow wood or with water, the reasoning depends on recognising a variety of situations as belonging to the same class. Ethics, like any other discourse, uses general terms that depend on the apprehension of such similarities. The whole of jurisprudence revolves around this, 'casuistry', as it was called. What counts as murder, what as manslaughter? Of course we have to lay down definitions, but whether a particular instance falls under one heading or another will always be contestable, even though some who professionally engage in such contestations may be accused by others of relying on 'spurious resemblances'.

Once again we find that while we can do without cross-species comparisons, the essential role of the recognition of similarities re-enters the picture at the intra-species level, that is what individuals or sub-species have in common. This is not the Aristotelian problem of how any induction can be perfect or complete, but the much more fundamental one of

---

[14] Cf. Lloyd (2004: 42) on *Hanfeizi* 36 (a text of the third century BCE). The general term for 'inconsistency' in classical Chinese is *bei*. But 'lances and shields' (*maodun*) came to be used as a way of referring metonymically to inconsistency.

[15] In the looser form of sorites the reasoner moves from one admission to a second similar one, on to a next and a next, to arrive at some conclusion. In many Chinese examples this was used positively to recommend that conclusion, though in Greece such arguments were sometimes used as a *reductio* to undermine a whole stretch of reasoning.

the justification of the use of any general term. In ethics we shall need a Chinese sage ruler, or an Aristotelian *phronimos*, or at least a person of common sense. The question of whether, in other fields of reasoning, we can dispense with appeal to the good judgement of the reasoner, is one that I shall take up again in the next chapter and in my Conclusions.

CHAPTER 4

Analogies as heuristic

Oportet enim nobis servire voces Geometricas analogiae; plurimum namque amo analogias, fidelissimos meos magistros, omnium naturae arcanorum conscios: in Geometria praecipue suspiciendos, dum infinitos casus interiectos intra sua extrema, mediumque, quantumvis absurdis locutionibus concludunt, totamque rei alicuius essentiam luculenter ponunt ob oculos.

(For us geometrical terms ought to obey analogy. For I love more than anything the analogies, my most trustworthy masters. They are aware of all the secrets of nature. In geometry especially they ought to be esteemed, for despite the incongruous terminology they resolve an infinity of cases between their extremes and the mean, and they place the whole essence of any subject vividly before the eyes.)

Kepler (1968 [1604]: ch. 4, 95)

My discussion of analogies in Greek and Chinese ethics has already brought to light first just how extensively they were used, secondly how warnings about their deceptiveness can be found in both Greek and Chinese writers, and thirdly that exceptionally, in Greece, Aristotle attempted an analysis of analogical argument explaining under what conditions it can be considered valid, namely where there is a complete induction of all the particular cases falling under a genus. That sets the agenda for this chapter where I focus on heuristics. There are some authoritative analyses of the use of analogies and models in modern science, notably the classic essay by Hesse on their role in the development of thermodynamics (Hesse 1963).[1] One particularly fruitful area for the exploration of analogies has been the use of computers to model complex cognitive processes, where the strengths of the positive

---

[1] Since Black (1962), Hesse (1963) and Lakoff and Johnson (1980) there has been an explosion of new research on the roles of analogies, models and metaphors in science. Two recent collective volumes will serve as an introduction to the massive literature in history and philosophy of science, developmental psychology and cognitive science on the subject, namely Gentner, Holyoak and Kokinov (2001) and Holyoak and Morrison (2005). Cf. also, for example, Miall (1982), Vosniadou and Ortony (1989) and Holyoak and Thagard (1995).

analogies have been such as to make problematic the question of whether we are dealing with 'mere' analogies. Does the computer have a mind, or does it just behave in ways that resemble one – the issue at the heart of controversies over Artificial Intelligence (e.g. Searle 1984, Haugeland 1985, Crane 1995), where the role of analogy in computational reasoning has been much studied (e.g. Kedar-Cabelli 1988, Burstein 1988, Holyoak and Thagard 1989)? Here, however, the chief topic I shall address relates to the ancient antecedents of the heuristic role or roles of analogies. One of my strategic aims, in these studies, is to examine the strengths and weaknesses of recurrent Western methodological preoccupations, in particular the insistence, in certain contexts at least, on strict deductive demonstration. Accordingly I shall, in this chapter, pay special attention to both the positive and the negative evaluations of analogy in heuristics that we find not just in ancient Greece, but also in ancient China and further afield.

Let me first outline the structure of my discussion. The first section will concentrate on mathematics and consider how the apprehension of similarities and the appeal to perceptible diagrams figure in a variety of contexts, and serve different purposes, in both China and Greece. One of the principal aims of early Chinese mathematics, at least to judge from remarks in Liu Hui in the third century CE,[2] is to establish the common features that link different members of the same class of mathematical objects and, further, to develop procedures that can be applied to different fields of mathematical studies, allowing the subject to grow by extrapolation. Liu Hui considers this to be research into the guiding principles of mathematics and he expresses no reservations on the matter. The contrast with Archimedes is striking, for he develops what he calls a mechanical method that depends on an implicit analogy between geometrical areas and volumes and physical bodies. However, he then insists that this is *just* a heuristic method and that the results must thereafter be demonstrated using the standard Greek techniques of the misnamed method of exhaustion,[3] and *reductio*. A method that is good for discovery is by itself not sufficient for demonstration. At the same time the demonstrative methods that we find in Euclid and in Archimedes himself rely heavily on diagrams, not analogies, to be sure, but icons or exemplars that stand in for the abstract relationships they represent.

[2] Liu Hui's is the first extant commentary on the Chinese mathematical classic, *Jiuzhang suanshu* (see Chemla and Guo 2004).
[3] One typical use of the 'method of exhaustion' was to determine a curvilinear area such as a circle by inscribing successively larger regular polygons (a technique used in Chinese as well as Greek mathematics). But the Greeks did not assume that the circle was indeed thereby exhausted, only that the difference between the inscribed polygon and the circle could be made as small as you like.

As a coda to my discussion of analogies in ancient mathematics I shall look at Kepler's praise of them, and his controversy with Robert Fludd over their legitimacy, in order to illustrate both their continuing importance and the ongoing disputes over their status.

My second section turns back to antiquity to where some more unreservedly positive attitudes towards analogy as heuristic are to be found, sometimes with, but sometimes without, some recognition of the dangers of unrestrained analogising. A variety of fifth- and fourth-century BCE Greek authors advocated using the 'phenomena' as a 'vision' of the 'obscure' (*opsis adēlōn ta phainomena*). That programme is not limited to suggesting analogies, but often involves finding or proposing such, while inevitably recognising differences between the items compared, the ones visible, the others invisible. That will take me into a discussion of just some of the uses of analogies in other societies, ancient and modern. In the Chinese case the apprehension of similarities and correspondences is a recurrent feature of the discussion of five-phase theory (*wu xing*). Many of those correspondences relate to physical properties, but we have also to take into account where they depend rather on symbolic associations or even on puns or wordplay.

I turn in the third section to Aristotle, whose criticisms of imagery and metaphor in definition and demonstration have been mentioned several times already. Yet a key concept he uses both in his metaphysics and in his zoology is a mode of resemblance where the similars are not the same in number, in species or in genus, but, precisely, by analogy (*tōi analogon*). Quite how this is to be squared with his general ideals for inquiry in the *Organon* will occupy the third section of the chapter.

That leads on to a fundamental issue that will occupy the rest of this chapter and the next, namely the presuppositions that are involved in the use of any general terms in any natural language insofar as they depend on the apprehension of a relationship of similarity between the items to which the term applies. Following up Aristotle's zoological analogies I shall explore this in relation to the key concept of 'animal'. What were assumed to be the defining characteristics of animals in either ancient Greek or ancient China? Was it always thought that animal kinds each had stable characteristics? How were the similarities and differences between animals and plants represented, and did reflection on that question lead to the expression of divergent views? Once again we may cross-reference modern research on the subject, though not in the expectation that that will necessarily provide definitive answers that settle questions that were beyond the reach of ancient thinkers. That will take me in Chapter 5 to an analysis of the general ontological issues and the extent to which we can or should allow for pluralism in the answers we give to this question of the objective bases for generalisations, and not just with regard to animals.

I

Proportion theory was already a subject of intense research in ancient Greece, where arithmetic, geometric and harmonic means were distinguished before Plato. Aristotle refers to the law that proportionals alternate, that is, that if A is to B as C is to D, then A is to C as B is to D, and says that this used to be established separately for numbers, lines, solids and periods of time. But by his day it had been realised that a single demonstration could be given to cover all those cases (*Posterior Analytics* 74a17–20). The first type of mathematical analogies I am concerned with here relates more generally to the apprehension of similarities across problems and indeed across areas of mathematical inquiry.

One of the chief aims of Chinese mathematics, at least to judge by what we find in Liu Hui, was to explore the unity of mathematics and to extend its range. Liu Hui comments that the same procedures provide the solutions to problems in different subject-areas. In his autobiographical introduction to his commentary on the *Nine Chapters* (91.6ff.) he says he looked for the guiding principles (*gangji*) of mathematics, that showed how the different branches of the subject all had the same root or trunk (*ben*), and have a single source or principle (*duan*). Two general procedures that he finds at work in different contexts are those he names 'homogenising' (*qi²*) and 'equalising' (*tong*). He exemplifies this in his discussion of the addition of fractions. 'Every time denominators multiply a numerator which does not correspond to them, we call this homogenise: multiplying with one another the set of denominators, we call this equalise' (96.1ff.). In adding the two fractions a/b and c/d we first 'homogenise' by multiplying a/b by d/d and c/d by b/b. We then 'equalise', using the fact that the multiplication of the denominators, b and d, allows the numerators to be added. So a/b + c/d = ad/bd + bc/bd = (ad + bc)/bd.

Now the terms *qi²* and *tong* are used in the text on which Liu Hui is commenting: they occur in the *Nine Chapters* at 1 18, 99.4 and 7, VII 14, 206.11–12, but it took Liu Hui himself to explain and define them and to draw attention to the way they provide a unifying thread across different problem areas. This extending of the same procedures across different categories (*lei*) makes the whole subject, according to Liu Hui, 'simple but precise, open to communication but not obscure'. Nor is this

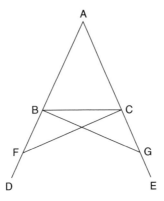

Diagram 1 Euclid, *Elements* 1 5.

just a particular feature of the discussion of the aims of mathematics in Liu Hui, since the other early mathematical classic from the turn of the millennium, the *Zhoubi suanjing* also says that 'it is the ability to distinguish categories (*lei*) in order to unite categories' which is the key to the subject (25.5). Among the methods that comprise the *Dao*, it is 'those which are concisely worded but of broad application that are the most illuminating of the categories of understanding. If one asks about one category and applies [this knowledge] to a myriad affairs, one is said to know the Way' (24.12ff.).

On the one hand, we may recognise that in his explanation of the various algorithms used in the *Nine Chapters* Liu Hui shows that they are correct: the 'procedures cannot have lost their original quantities' as he puts it in his discussion of the addition of fractions (96.1–2). On the other, he shows no signs of expecting or demanding that the whole of mathematics, indeed any part of it, should be put on an axiomatic basis. As I noted before (p. 51) that kind of demonstration is simply not on his agenda, nor on that of any Chinese mathematician until the Jesuits informed them that their notions of proving were inadequate. The aim of classical Chinese mathematics was not to give incontrovertible axiomatic-deductive demonstrations but to expand the subject by extrapolation, that is by extending the procedures used to more and more cases. Analogies provide the links that enable this growth. The aim is heuristics, then, rather than the one that many Greek mathematicians set themselves, namely such Euclidean demonstrations.

We are all familiar with the way the *Elements* proceeds, first setting out the definitions, postulates and common opinions needed and then proceeding to the rigorous demonstration of theorems or solutions to problems of

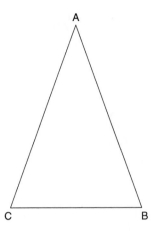

Diagram 2 Alternative Proof of Euclid, 1 5.

construction. Now on the one hand, as Netz (1999) showed, the actual demonstrations we are typically given in Greek geometry crucially depend on the construction of the diagram, built up in an orderly sequence in which the points referred to generally follow the order of the letters of the Greek alphabet. How does one of the earliest proofs in the *Elements*, that of the equality of the base angles of an isosceles triangle (1 5), work? It uses the diagram with which we are all familiar in which the equalities are shown via appeal to the similarities of triangles.[4] Actually it was not necessary to proceed in that manner. One can do the job on a single triangle, imagining it as double.[5] Triangle ABC is congruent with triangle ACB (the angle at the apex is common and the sides are equal) so it follows that angle ABC is equal to angle ACB. But in practice Euclid uses the construction I have set out, which evidently provides a visual prompt for the exploration of the geometrical relations. In that context the perceptible diagram certainly plays an important heuristic role, even though the geometry is not about perceptibles, but about the geometrical relations themselves.

Similarly in the demonstration of what we know as Pythagoras' theorem, the familiar 'windmill' diagram, as constructed, enables the equalities of the areas in question to be shown.[6] That example is interesting because it

---

[4] Diagram for Euclid, *Elements* 1 5. Diagram 1. AF is made equal to AG. So $\triangle$ AFC is similar to $\triangle$ AGB. So FC = GB and A^FC = A^GB and A^BG = A^CF. Now $\triangle$ BFC = $\triangle$ BGC, and F^BC = G^CB and B^CF = C^BG. So invoking the equality axiom (take equals from equals and equals remain) A^BG – C^BG = A^CF – B^CF. In other words A^BC equals A^CB.

[5] Alternative proof of Euclid, *Elements* 1 5. Diagram 2.

[6] Diagram for proof of Pythagoras' theorem, Euclid, *Elements* 1 47. Diagram 3.

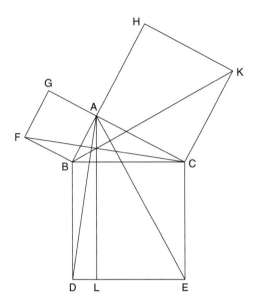

Diagram 3 Euclid, *Elements* I 47.

brings to light differences in the way in which diagrams are used in different ancient geometrical traditions, Indian as well as Chinese. Although the original diagrams have not been preserved,[7] we know from references to them that they figured in the discussion of the properties of the right-angled triangle. Neither the Indian *Āpastamba Śulbasūtra* nor the Chinese *Nine Chapters* speaks of theorems, but both were well aware that in a right-angled triangle, the square on the hypotenuse (called *xian* in Chinese) is equal to that of the squares on the other two sides, where the Chinese used *gou* for the horizontal, and *gu* for the vertical line enclosing the right angle.

---

[7] They have indeed been reconstructed very differently by ancient and modern commentators. Qu 1997 gives one possible reconstruction of the diagram used in *gou gu* studies in the *Zhoubi suanjing* (Diagram 4, with Qu's version of the steps by which the shapes were manipulated). The starting-point (6a) is a big square with sides 4 + 3, giving a total area of 49 units. The bottom left 'red' rectangle (sides 4 and 3) is moved to the right and rotated 90°, and moved and rotated twice more, to give the array shown in 6c, where the area of the square on the hypotenuse can be got as 25 units. From the original 49 units are subtracted four triangles (marked red in 6c), each of which has an area 6, being half of the corresponding rectangle with sides 4 and 3. So 49 − 24 gives 25, which in turn is equal to the squares on the two smaller sides (4 and 3). Chemla and Guo (2004: 674ff.) (among others) have reported several other reconstructions, but all depend on knowledge that in a right-angled triangle where the shorter sides are 3 and 4 units respectively, the hypotenuse will be 5 units in length.

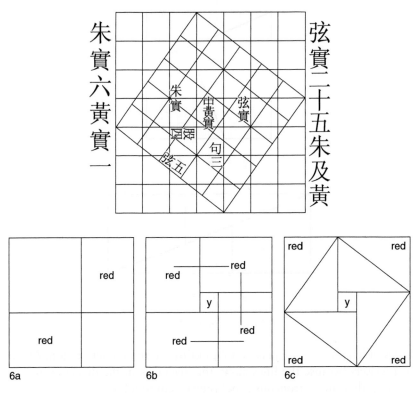

Diagram 4 Qu's reconstruction of *gou gu* diagram and of its construction.

However, the Chinese showed that result not by an axiomatic-deductive demonstration such as is carefully built up in Euclid, but rather by the manipulation of areas, in a procedure they called the Out–In Complementary Principle (*churu xiangbu*). This is a kind of scissors and paste technique, which is also used in Greek geometry, but only very occasionally since it certainly did not meet their usual standards of proof. But whether the figures so constructed are indeed squares, whether the angles are right, whether the lines joining the segments are indeed straight, is not shown but assumed. In that context the diagrams are *simply* heuristic, not a tool in a method of axiomatic-deductive demonstration.

Indeed that underestimates the problem, for diagrams may not only be merely suggestive, they may positively mislead. A well-known paradox, a favourite with Lewis Carroll, exemplifies how a certain manipulation of unit squares might look as if it gives the conclusion that the square on the

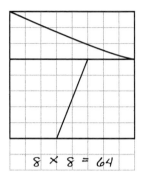

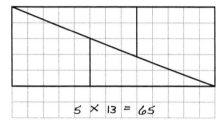

Diagram 5 Sam Loyd's puzzle.

sides of lengths 3 + 5 equals not 64 but 65, or, in another version, 63.[8] It is precisely because the lines along the diagonals in the diagrams are *not* straight that these erroneous conclusions seem to follow.

So this takes me to some of the criticisms levelled at the use of diagrams in the Greek tradition itself, and first and foremost of course to Plato's discussion, in the *Republic*, of how the mathematicians proceed. It is especially ironic that Plato, himself a past master in the use of images, should make these comments on mathematics in a text that itself explores the Form of the Good by way of three analogies, the Sun, the Divided Line and the Cave, where Socrates excuses himself by saying that he cannot give a direct account of the Good, only one of its 'offspring'. In the second of these images the reasoning of the mathematicians is said to be an example of what is there called *dianoia*, the second-highest section in the Line, contrasted with the top one, *noēsis*, which leads up to the apprehension of the Form of the Good itself.

[8] An ancestor of the puzzle appears already in Hooper (1794: 286). Sam Loyd the elder claimed that he presented the paradox to the American Chess Congress in 1858, where the rearrangement of the square of side 8 appears to give the result 65 (see Gardner 1956: 133), Diagram 5, and his son, also called Sam Loyd, discovered the assemblage that gives the result 63, Diagram 6. For Lewis Carroll's interest see Fisher (1973: 92ff.). Cf. also Denyer (2007).

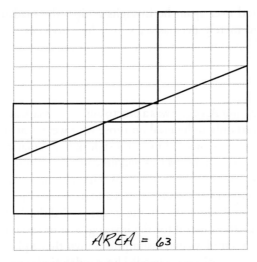

AREA = 63

Diagram 6 Sam Loyd Junior's variation.

The two features of mathematical methods that Socrates focuses on (*Republic* 510cd) are first the use of visible images, and second their failure to give an account of their assumptions. He recognises that the mathematicians are not concerned with the perceptible features of those diagrams, but rather with the geometrical properties themselves, the 'square itself', 'the diagonal itself', for instance. But there is absolutely no explicit recognition of the positive heuristic role that the diagrams themselves may fulfil. Nor is the criticism that the mathematicians give no account of their assumptions exactly on target. The mathematicians take their principles to be 'clear to anyone',[9] but insofar as they are indeed self-evident, one may wonder what further justification they need, or could be given.

Plato's assessment of mathematics in the *Republic* is skewed first of all by his preoccupation with the contrast between perceptible particulars and intelligible Forms. But in his general evaluations of modes of reasoning he is further obsessed by the contrast he drew between persuasion and

[9] Quite how this phrase is to be taken is disputed. Some have maintained that as the principles are indeed clear, this is the warrant the mathematicians can appeal to in order to justify their procedures (e.g. Vlastos 1991: 130). But observing that some of the principles that ancient mathematicians used, such as straight line and point, were indeed disputed, I read this not as their warrant, but rather as their claim (Lloyd 1991: ch. 14, 340). A further point at issue is whether Plato meant this as a criticism of the mathematicians. Burnyeat (2000: 37) remarked that since the mathematicians are compelled to use visible diagrams, it would be harsh to pillory them for doing so. Yet Plato evidently downgrades their procedures in comparison with those of the philosophers when they seek to grasp the Form of the Good itself.

proof. Over and over again he inveighs against the inadequacy of arguments that are merely persuasive, which he associates particularly with
those generally used by sophists and politicians, in law-courts and political
assemblies. As we have seen, his ideal, and that of Aristotle after him, was
to secure the truth with arguments that could claim to be certain, indeed
incontrovertible.

Neither Plato nor Aristotle was a practising mathematician, but that ideal
of theirs was certainly influential on those who were, starting with Euclid
and including all those who adopted his style of mathematical proof. While
Greek mathematicians themselves had no compunction in using diagrams
in their proofs, some of the most famous ones were nevertheless very much
aware of the contrast between heuristics and demonstration. I am thinking
now, of course, of Archimedes. In the treatise called the *Method* he sets out
a mechanical method useful for the investigation of certain mathematical
problems.[10] This employs two assumptions, first that a plane figure can be
imagined as made up of a set of parallel lines indefinitely close together, and,
secondly, that these lines can be thought of as balanced by corresponding
lines of the same magnitude in a figure of known area. The first theorem,
he says, that he discovered by this method is that which gives the area of
a parabolic segment as four-thirds that of a triangle with the same base
and height. He first sets out how the method works in such an example,
but then both in the *Method* and in the *Quadrature of the Parabola* he
proceeds to give a proof using the standard techniques of exhaustion and
reductio, evidently because, as he says,[11] the mechanical method itself does
not constitute – for him – a demonstration.

Now both the assumptions on which the method depends breach basic
principles generally taken for granted in Greek mathematics. The assumption that a plane figure can be taken to be constituted by a set of indivisible
line segments flies in the face of the usual Greek view that geometry
deals with an infinitely divisible continuum. If the line segments have any
breadth, they cannot be treated as lines. But if they are imagined as of zero
breadth, summing them will lead to zero – the problem only resolved with
the explicit theorems on which the integral calculus is based. Similarly,
to imagine that mathematical figures have centres of gravity breaches a
second fundamental principle, namely the categorical distinction between
mathematical objects and physical ones.

[10] Archimedes, *Method* Heiberg–Stamatis II 428.18ff.
[11] Archimedes, *Method* II 428.28–9; the inquiry by means of this method is 'without a demonstration'.

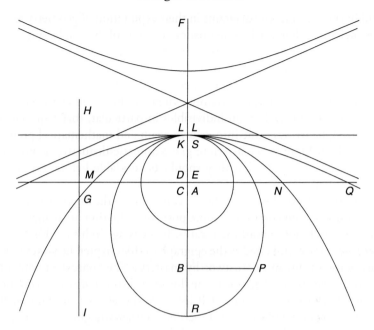

Diagram 7 Kepler, *Paralipomena to Witelo*, ch. 4.

No doubt these were considerations that weighed with Archimedes when he explicitly denied that the method is demonstrative, even though others might have taken it that it showed the truth of the theorems in question quite adequately and did not just facilitate their discovery. The use of indivisibles was not vindicated until the revival of mathematics in the seventeenth century with Cavalieri, by which time the value of analogies in geometry was feted by Kepler among others, as I shall be considering in a moment (cf. Polya 1954a).

But we should note that Archimedes' own reasons for caution have nothing to do with any Platonic inhibition about the use of perceptible diagrams. He has no quarrel with them, for he would be under no illusions as to their role in, precisely, the construction of Greek geometrical proofs. Nevertheless the *Method* shows very clearly that the ideal in parts of Greek mathematics (at least) was that demonstrations in the Euclidean axiomatic-deductive mode should be given wherever possible.

As I have argued on previous occasions,[12] it was at that point that some Greek mathematics is quite exceptional. Although the Greeks were as

---

[12] For example Lloyd (1979: ch. 2, 1996a: ch. 3, 2012c).

skilful in the use of iconic diagrams in their exploration of geometry as any other ancient mathematicians, heuristics, for some of them at least, was not enough. Yet there was a price to pay for this, for although we cannot detail this, it is clear that some Greek mathematicians would have been inhibited from publishing their results when they were unable to provide these with canonical demonstrations. Certainly, when in the seventeenth century, with the work of Cavalieri on indivisibles in particular, that requirement was relaxed, heuristics came into its own again and mathematical progress ceased to be held up by a concern to give axiomatic-deductive demonstrations, indeed to require that they should be available before any results were published.

As an appendix to this section let me comment on the ongoing tension in Kepler himself, who combines a more positive evaluation of analogies with continued hesitations about their status. In a passage in his *Ad Vitellionem Paralipomena*, which I cited as the epigraph of this chapter, he waxes lyrical in his praise of 'his most trustworthy masters'. The context in which he does so is indeed a mathematical one, his investigation of conic sections.[13] The sections of cones, he says, fall into five species, for the line on the surface of a cone established by a section is either straight, or a circle, or a parabola or hyperbola or ellipse, and these form a sequence. This starts with the straight line (though in that case there is no actual section), passes through an infinity of hyperbolas to the parabola, and thence through an infinity of ellipses to the circle. In each case one of their centres is called the 'focus' (from an analogy with light), the line that marks out the focus on the axis, perpendicular to the axis, is named the 'chord' (not the usual use of that term), while the line that gives the altitude of the focus from the vertex is called the 'sagitta' ('arrow'), and he sets about calculating the proportions of those last two for each type of conic section.[14]

In this context he has no reservations about the analogies since the five types of sections can be treated as species of a single genus exhibiting analogous properties. There is then a proportionality between them

[13] In his 1604 he uses Diagram 7, where the straight line he is interested in is LL, the parabola GKN and the infinity of hyperbolas lying between them is represented by LQ. The line MN that marks out the focus on the axis is the 'chord', while the 'sagitta' is BR or DK or ES for the ellipse, parabola and hyperbola respectively.
[14] In the circle the sagitta is equal to half the 'chord'; in the ellipse the half-chord BP is greater than the sagitta BR; in the parabola the sagitta DK is exactly equal to a quarter of the chord MN; in the hyperbola EQ is more than twice the sagitta ES, that is ES is less than one quarter of the chord EQ and 'is ever less and less . . . until it vanishes in the straight line, where, the focus falling directly upon the line, the altitude of the focus, or the sagitta, vanishes, and the chord at the same time is made infinite since it coincides with its own arc'. At that point Kepler adds that this is to speak improperly, since the arc is a straight line (Kepler 1968 [1604]: 94–5, Donahue 2000: 109).

('analogia' in the strictest sense of proportion). Yet elsewhere in his frequent proposals of analogies, now in the looser sense of similarities,[15] between physics and mathematics or within physics or again between cosmology and epistemology, he acknowledges their heuristic or conjectural character, where he is as clear as Plato had been about the gap between a strict demonstration and a (mere) conjecture.

This comes out, for example, in his controversy with the Rosicrucian Robert Fludd (almost his exact contemporary) to which he devotes an appendix to book 5 of his *Harmonices Mundi* (*The Harmony of the World*). Fludd had criticised Kepler on the grounds that he did not appreciate the real connections between the microcosm and the macrocosm (which were the basis of Fludd's own practice as an astrologer). But Kepler countered that Fludd's astrological influences were ill-founded. Fludd found analogies between the three worlds he distinguished, the 'empyrean', the celestial and the terrestrial, but according to Kepler these analogies were merely symbolic, just as he criticised Ptolemy's cosmic harmonies in book III of his *Harmonics* as merely poetic and rhetorical, 'rather than philosophical or mathematical' (Kepler 1940 [1619]: 374). Kepler himself, by contrast, claimed that his own cosmic analogies were based on his determination of the motions and distances of the planets themselves, on quantitative data, in other words, rather than merely qualitative associations. It was that observational basis that, for him, justified both his finding the five regular solids in the cosmos and his views on the harmonic relations between the planets, as well as his own particular ideas about astrological influences.

As for their disagreements on harmonic theory itself, Kepler put it that harmonies 'are never to be sought when the things between which the harmonies are cannot be measured by the same quantitative measure' – as, for example, between two lengths of string of the same tension. I have shown, he wrote (1619: 372, Aiton, Duncan and Field 1997: 503) 'that in the heaven according to true and quantitative reasoning, and based on measurement, but not by mere trivial interpretation of symbols, there are all the harmonic proportions, the kinds of harmonies, the musical system or scale, and most of its keys, the varieties of tones, planets which emulate the figured music of voices, and finally the universal counterpoints of the six primary planets, varying both in kinds and in tones'.

[15] Among his more notable analogies are those between reflection and refraction, between light and magnetism, and especially between the motions of the planets and harmonies: these have been discussed by, for example, Buchdahl (1972) and by Vickers (1984), although Vickers is in general overeager to drive a wedge between what he calls the 'occult' and the 'scientific' 'mentalities', in particular in the matter of treating analogies as identities.

Some of Kepler's analogies could, he claimed, be vindicated as being between items that belong to a single determinate genus, and others have an empirical basis. Yet while he was critical of others' uncontrolled analogising, he proposes some highly speculative analogies himself. One of his boldest comes in the same work, the *Harmony of the World*, in which he criticised Fludd. Kepler himself compares the relationship between the six planetary spheres and the centre of the universe to that between *dianoia* and *nous*, that is between discursive reason and intellect, a distinction he finds in 'Aristotle, Plato, Proclus and others'. However, he explicitly labelled this chapter 'conjectural', and he introduces his suggestion with the guarded remark 'it would not be absurd for someone to suggest'. Like so many before him, and indeed many after him, right down to the present day, when faced with what he calls the mysteries of nature he 'follows the thread of analogy'.[16] While such fully elaborated four-term proportional analogies are not so common, similarities, as we shall confirm, are basic to every field of inquiry and indeed to every mode of cognition.

II

We have an explicit formula that could be used to promote physical analogies in the ancient Greek dictum that 'phenomena' are the 'vision' of the 'obscure', a saying attributed to Anaxagoras and said to have been approved by Democritus.[17] Although we do not have Democritus' own statements of his theory but have to depend on reports of it, we can see that the properties of geometrical shapes are used to explain or at least to conjecture those of the atoms and of the compounds they form. An acid flavour (*oxu*, sharp), for instance, was ascribed to atoms that are 'angular', small and thin, according to Theophrastus (*On the Senses* 65ff.). Then in quite a number of fifth- and fourth-century writers we have fairly clear echoes of the dictum itself.

---

[16] Kepler (1940 [1619]: book 5, ch. 10, 366). Cf. Aiton, Duncan and Field (1997: 495f.): 'But if we may follow the thread of analogy and pass through the labyrinths of the mysteries of nature, it would not, I think, be absurd for someone to argue that the disposition of the six spheres towards their common centre, and therefore the centre of the whole world, is the same as that of "thought" [*dianoia*] to "mind"[*nous*]'.

[17] This is reported in Sextus Empiricus, *Against the Mathematicians* (7:140); cf. Diller (1932). In assessing the diverse Greek ideas concerning the investigability of nature, a balance needs to be struck. In a recent study, Hadot (2006), starting from Heraclitus' dictum that 'nature loves to hide' (Fr. 123), puts the emphasis on the theme of the obscurities of nature, whose secrets have to be unveiled. But in the echoes of the Anaxagorean dictum that I consider in my text, the stress is rather on the possibility of the *vision* of the obscure that appearances can provide.

Herodotus provides a particularly clear example in his discussion of the course of the Nile (2.33–4). An expedition led by Etearchus across Africa had found a great river which Herodotus conjectured to be the Nile, partly on the basis of the analogy with the Danube, the course of which he says is known, since it flows through inhabited country. Europe and Africa, he believes, both have major rivers of about the same length running across them, so, 'inferring things that are not known from things that are plain', Herodotus conjectures that the river Etearchus found was indeed the Nile (when it may well have been the Niger). It is striking that elsewhere (4.36, cf. 42) Herodotus ridicules earlier Greek geographers who had assumed that the world is symmetrical and made Asia and Europe of equal size. Yet he too relies on an assumed analogy between his two great rivers to arrive at this conclusion, while emphasising, to be sure, that this was just a conjecture.

Analogies obviously prove particularly useful at points where confirmation by direct observation is not possible, yet where that was the case the analogies were indeed just conjectures. One of the chief contexts in which we find them relates to the internal processes and structures in the human body, where Hippocratic writers of the fifth and fourth centuries BCE used them extensively, as I discussed in Lloyd (1966: 345–59).[18] One particularly striking example again contains an echo of the Anaxagorean dictum.

In *On Ancient Medicine* ch. 22 (*CMG* I 1, 53.1–54.24) the writer lists the different structures or forms of the parts of the body: some are hollow and tapering, some 'spread out', some hard and round, some broad and drawn out, some stretched, some long, some dense, some loose and swollen, some spongy and porous. But asking which type of structure is best adapted to draw fluid to itself he answers that it is the tapering and hollow one: 'one should learn these things outside the body from objects that are plain to see' (in this case his chief analogue is cupping instruments). So he believes that the bladder, the head and the womb, which are all of this general shape, will have that property. On the one hand, analogies from outside the body are evidently a rich source of ideas about what may happen inside it. On the other, everything depends, of course, on whether the analogy holds in the respect in question. Analogies may be the only method possible where direct observation cannot be made: but the very lack of such verification is their greatest weakness.

In fact the history of speculative thought – and not just in antiquity – is strewn with examples where every type of similarity was exploited to

---

[18] Among the problems on which such analogies were brought to bear were the effects of drugs inside the body, the interaction of humours and the development of the embryo.

make some connection between things, whether that was taken to be just
a symbolic association, or indeed a causal one. I noted in the Introduction that in medieval Europe the Doctrine of Signatures maintained that
every natural substance carried indications of the disease for which they
were remedies, or indeed which they caused. Much of what was labelled
'sympathetic magic' depended on what Frazer called the Law of Similarity
or on the Law of Contact or Contagion (Frazer 1911–15 I: ch. 3),[19] though
Tambiah, for one, was to insist that much ritual behaviour should be seen
less as attempting to be efficacious, than as affective or expressive. The criteria that are relevant to assessing such behaviour are, then, not whether it
produces practical results, but whether it has been carried out appropriately
or not. Citing Austin (1962), Tambiah focused on the performative or illo-
cutionary force of magical actions, which should then be judged from the
point of view of their felicity, rather than from that of their effectiveness.[20]

As has often been pointed out, again notably by Tambiah (1968, 1973),
language itself can play a crucial role in such performances, where the
similarities in question may be a matter of similarities in the *names* of
things. They depend, therefore, on wordplay or puns, as has been discussed
in relation to Mesopotamian texts, especially medical ones, by Livingstone
(1986) and by Geller (2010), and in relation to astrological practice by
Rochberg (2004). While the search for similarities via an examination of
language is widespread, clearly the particular connections identified depend
on the particular natural language in question. One further culturally
specific practice comes from ancient Greece. The Greeks used the letters
of their alphabet as the symbols for numbers, alpha for 1, beta for 2,
gamma for 3 and so on. But that means that any name for a person or a
thing can be connected with a particular number, simply by adding up the
values of the constituent letters. It is of course not the case that all Greeks
believed that there is a profound significance in such associations, but some
certainly did, even while others criticised them as fantastical, as Aristotle
was to condemn much of the number symbolism of the early Pythagoreans
when he attacked the view that numbers are the first principles of things
in a splendid tirade in the last chapter of the *Metaphysics* 1093a3–28. It
so happens, he there says, that there are seven vowels (in Greek), seven
strings to the lyre, and seven stars in the Pleiades (though some say there
are more), and even that most animals (but not all) lose their teeth in the

---

[19] We may compare Lévy-Bruhl's notion that primitive thought is governed not by the Laws of
Contradiction and Excluded Middle, but rather by what he called a law of participation (Lévy-
Bruhl 1926).

[20] Tambiah (1973: 220ff.; cf. 1990: ch. 1).

seventh year, and that the heroes who fought against Thebes were seven in number. But in none of these cases does the explanation lie in the number seven. Aristotle, of course, demands a causal account, not a mere parade of accidental correspondences.

I may now extend this part of my discussion of the wider contexts of the use of similarities by quoting one of the most influential studies of magic, that of Evans-Pritchard on the Azande (1937: 486f.). First he puzzled over whether the Zande name for mumps relied simply on a verbal analogy, for that name incorporated the word used for a particular kind of bird, a small finch, that has a lump on its neck. But he then went on to say that was probably the case:

> For we know that in primitive patterns of thought objects which have a superficial resemblance are often linked up by nomenclature and ritual and are connected in mystical patterns of thought. In Zande therapeutics this mystical connexion is found in notions about cause and cure. Ringworm resembles in appearance fowls' excrement, and fowls' excrement is at the same time both cause and cure of ringworm. Blepharoptosis resembles a hen's egg, and a hen's egg is its cure. Generally the logic of therapeutic treatment consists in the selection of the most prominent external symptoms, the naming of the disease after some object in nature it resembles, and the utilization of the object as the principal ingredient in the drug administered to cure the disease. The circle may even be completed by belief that the symptoms not only yield to treatment by the object which resembles them, but are caused by it as well.

Evans-Pritchard was in general confident that he could draw distinctions between 'mystical notions', 'common-sense notions' and 'scientific notions'.[21] But if we turn back to our other main ancient civilisation, China, we can see how very much more complicated the problem is than Evans-Pritchard imagined. There was no Chinese Anaxagoras to suggest that 'the phenomena are the vision of the obscure',[22] but their explorations

---

[21] Evans-Pritchard (1937: 12): 'Mystical notions. These are patterns of thought that attribute to phenomena supra-sensible qualities which, or part of which, are not derived from observation or cannot be logically inferred from it, and which they do not possess. Common-sense notions. These are patterns of thought that attribute to phenomena only what men observe in them or what can logically be inferred from observation . . . Scientific notions. Science has developed out of common sense but is far more methodical and has better techniques of observation and reasoning. Common sense uses experience and rules of thumb. Science uses experiment and rules of Logic.'

[22] Strikingly, when in *Huainanzi* we find a chapter devoted to 'examining obscurities' (*lanming* 6: 3a), the emphasis is on the mutual resonances of things which are described as mysterious and unfathomable: 'knowledge is not capable of assessing it, argument is not able to explain it. When the east wind blows, wine turns clear and spills over'. You need, in fact, to be a sage to be able to grasp this, but the sage is like a mirror: he responds but he does not retain (6: 6b).

Diagram 8 Hexagram 27 *Yi*.

of the parallelisms and correspondences between different things are both wide-ranging and methodical.

The two main contexts in which they engaged in this are the *Yijing* or *Book of Changes*, some parts of which may go all the way back to the ninth century BCE, and in relation to five-phase theory. In the former the individual practitioners manipulated piles of sticks of milfoil or yarrow to give an array, a hexagram, constituted by six broken or unbroken lines. But from that point on, the interpretation of each line and each group of them, both in their original configuration and in their various transforms, was a matter of using but also adapting whatever the traditional Commentaries offered by way of clues as to significances, sometimes, though not always, based on obvious analogies, sometimes on more recondite associations. Each line had a cryptic gloss and the lessons to be drawn from each hexagram as a whole were equally opaque and open-ended. Of course what the *Yijing* was used for varied, for this might be a matter of foreseeing the outcome of a course of action, or negotiating human relations, all the way to understanding the mysteries of the universe. This was not the only divinatory practice that was used to help remove doubts or to instil caution in dangerous or perplexing situations. But throughout, the interpretation of combinations of lines as suggestive of particular conclusions depended on extended chains of association.[23]

As regards five-phase theory, which I have mentioned before, this provided a framework within which a vast array of phenomena of different types could be ordered and so understood: animals, flavours, smells, emotions, musical notes, colours, cardinal points, seasons, all the way to

[23] Thus Hexagram 27 (in the traditional numbering), named *Yi*[2], is formed by unbroken lines at the top and at the bottom, with four broken lines in between, which suggests the gloss 'Jaws' or in another view 'Corners of the Mouth' (Diagram 8). This in turn is associated with 'providing nourishment' and further in line 5 from the bottom, with 'perseverance, which brings Good Fortune', because 'if one provides nourishment for what is right, good fortune comes'. However, one of the other lines (the broken one in the third place from the bottom) is glossed as 'acting contrary to nourishing'. This will lead to misfortune or evil. Evidently this leaves a good deal of room for manoeuvre in the interpretation of the hexagram as a whole on any particular occasion. The ancient and modern literature on interpretations of the *Changes*, is immense and highly divergent both in general and on specifics. Shaughnessy (1997) provides a sensible introduction.

political institutions.[24] The question that this poses is how to interpret all the correspondences that are proposed. Is it assumed that there are causal connections linking the items thus associated? Or should we see those connections as merely symbolic, to be assessed not in terms of efficacy but in those of appropriateness or felicity? It would seem that our answer must combine both elements. The very comprehensiveness of the tables of correlations may serve to give them a certain plausibility, but it is not the case that there was anything like total uniformity among different Chinese thinkers about what goes with what.

That causal considerations are sometimes, at least, in mind is clear in a number of texts. 'Things within the same class (*lei*) mutually move one another', as *Huainanzi* 3: 2b9, puts it, giving the interactions of root and twig as its first example. Resonances, conversely, show that the items that resonate belong to the same class, as in the case where striking one note causes the harmonic to sound. One of the examples in this chapter of *Huainanzi* is that of a burning-mirror which ignites tinder 'when it sees the sun'. Another is (as the Greeks also knew) that shellfish respond to the waxing and waning of the moon, but *Huainanzi* also has tigers resonating with winds and dragons with rain. It is, however, worth remarking that these interests in correspondences later led the Chinese to recognise the directionality of magnetised iron, the 'south-pointing needle' that is the origin of the compass. The Greeks knew about the attractive properties of the 'Magnetic' stone, but never spotted the correlation between its movements and the north/south axis.

Again we see tentative causal connections in play in the way in which the mutual conquest cycle is used by the second-century BCE doctor Chunyu Yi (as reported in the *Shiji*, in ch. 105). In one of the case-histories he describes (case 15: *Shiji* 105: 2806–7, Lloyd 1996a: 112), where he diagnoses an injured spleen, he predicts the blocking of the diaphragm when spring comes,

---

[24] Phase correlations appear in many different variants in classical Chinese texts and the tables of such given in the secondary literature (e.g. Needham 1956) often elide the differences in the original sources. But to follow one particularly detailed exposé, in *Huainanzi* 3–5, the phase Wood is associated with the East, the planet Year-Star (Jupiter), the colour blue-green, the liver, wheat, the flavour sour, the door-god to whom sacrifices should be made, and the ministry of agriculture; the next phase, Fire, goes with the South, the planet Sparkling Deluder (Mars), the colour red, the heart, rice, the flavour acrid, the stove-god and the ministry of war; and so on for the other three phases Earth, Metal and Water. One recurrent difficulty was to divide the seasons into five to correlate with the phases. One way was to partition the year into five periods of 72 days. Another (in the *Monthly Ordinances, Huainanzi* 5, cf. *Lüshi chunqiu* 6) was to assign three months each to Wood (spring), Metal (autumn) and Water (winter), but to allot only two summer months to Fire and the remaining one ('midsummer') to Earth. The problem of correlating four cardinal directions with the five phases was solved by counting the Centre (correlated with Earth) as a fifth point of reference.

followed by the passing of blood and death in the summer. The stomach
qi^1, he reports, was yellow, and that is the qi^1 of Earth. But Earth cannot
overcome Wood (in the mutual conquest cycle Wood overcomes Earth).
So when spring comes (spring being associated with Wood) there will be
death, though that was delayed for a season in this case because the patient
was contented and fat. Of course you had to know all the associations
that went with five-phase theory. But armed with those correlations, you
could provide explanations of a sort for a great variety of phenomena, even
though you had also to be prepared for partial exceptions.

At the same time we find some Chinese expressions of the idea that it
was a mistake to try and explain everything, whether by using analogies or
in any other way. A story in the *Zhuangzi* compilation makes the point,
when Zhuangzi criticises his friend and sparring partner Hui Shi.

> There was a stranger in the South called Huang Liao, who asked why heaven
> did not collapse nor earth subside, and the reasons (*gu*) for wind, rain and
> thunder. Hui Shi answered without hesitation, replied without thinking,
> had explanations (*shuo*) for all the myriad things, never stopped explaining,
> said more and more and still thought he had not said enough, had some
> marvel to add. (*Zhuangzi* 33: 81–3, trans. after Graham 1989: 77, Lloyd 1996a:
> 113–14)

As Zhuangzi puts it elsewhere (33: 84–7, Lloyd 1996a: 163) 'what a pity Hui
Shi's talents were wasted and never came to anything, that he would not
turn back from chasing the myriad things . . . Sad wasn't it?'

So Chinese ambitions to give causal explanations were sometimes more
circumscribed than those of the Presocratic philosophers or Hippocratic
writers – though not of Greeks of a more sceptical persuasion. What should
Hui Shi's talents have been directed towards? Zhuangzi puts the emphasis
on self-cultivation. But the answer that many Chinese would have given
would have been good government, and this takes me back to the felicity
aspect of the correlations proposed whether in *wu xing* theory or outside
it. Several texts known as the Monthly Ordinances (*yue ling*) set out the
appropriate behaviour for each month of the year. We have one example
in the opening books of the *Lüshi chunqiu* which describes the positions of
the constellations in each month, the weather anticipated, the behaviour
of animals and the like. But it also sets out the colour of the clothes the
Son of Heaven should wear, the food he should eat, where in the palace he
should reside, the music to be played.[25]

---

[25] In another version of the Monthly Ordinances, in *Huainanzi* 5, the recommendations extend to
the colour of the dresses to be worn by the court ladies.

The concern is that everything should be done appropriately, a matter of felicity, then, though the recommendations are followed up by dire warnings about the calamities if the proper rituals are not observed. 'If in the first month of autumn, the ordinances for winter are put into effect, *yin qi*[1] will prevail, scaly insects will destroy the harvest, and aggressive armies will be bound to invade' (*Lüshi chunqiu* 7/1/6). Cause–effect relations as well as looser correlations are clearly presupposed, both physical ones and human, political ones, but the chief motive of the authors responsible for such texts was clearly to influence, indeed to try to control, the ruler, for which a great display of claimed superior knowledge was mobilised, indeed a glittering manifestation of what Descola called 'dizzying analogism'.

III

But if analogies can be the source of, among other things, conjectures concerning what is puzzling or beyond observation, they are, of course, just analogies and we have already seen how doubts about deceptive similarities are expressed by both Greeks and Chinese. It is all the more remarkable that Aristotle, who is so critical of metaphor in the context of definition, and of analogy in the context of syllogistic, should nevertheless have made considerable use of the relationship of sameness 'by analogy' in both his metaphysics and his zoology. My next task is to explore further this apparent trace of a certain ambivalence towards analogy on his part.

The first difficulty can be easily stated. Each branch of understanding has, as Aristotle insists (*Posterior Analytics* 75a42–b2), its own genus, and the demonstrations it aims at have their own proper principles, which include definitions. He distinguishes between different types of definition in the *Posterior Analytics* ii ch. 10, including verbal definitions which simply explain the meanings of terms. However, his preferred modes are where the definition grasps the essence of what is defined, the standard form of which is by way of a genus and its differentiae (96b32–97a6). For valid deduction of any kind, as we have seen, the terms must be used univocally and the premises that yield demonstrative syllogisms have to meet the strict requirements he set out in *Posterior Analytics* i, ch. 2: that is, they must be primary, immediate, better known than, prior to and explanatory of the conclusions.

But if sameness and oneness by analogy *transcend* the genus, as in both metaphysical and zoological uses, how does that not breach those requirements? How can there be understanding in the strict sense Aristotle has defined, if that is limited to a determinate genus? How can there be demonstrations, if these are supposedly limited to the principles proper to the given branch of understanding? How can there be deduction, even, if the analogical use of terms departs from the strict model of predication he normally insists on? How can there be definitions, on which understanding depends and by means of which it is attained, if definition requires a proper genus to be differentiated?

Take his discussion of potentiality and actuality in *Metaphysics Theta* 1048a35–b4, where he makes it clear that this pair cannot be defined by way of a genus and differentiae. Rather we should grasp the analogy, he says. Just as what is actually building is to what is capable of building, so that which is awake is to that which is asleep, or that which is seeing to what has the faculty of sight but has its eyes closed, or that which has been worked up to what is not yet worked up. Here he recommends grasping the analogy in lieu of attempting a standard definition.

Of course potentiality and actuality do not constitute a proper subject-matter for a *specific* branch of understanding or the topic of demonstrations aimed at in such, such as those required in geometry, arithmetic and harmonics, for instance. So while the analysis of potentiality and actuality fails the *Posterior Analytics* tests of having a determinate subject genus, there was never any question that they should have had to pass those tests in the first place.

Yet notice what has happened. Here is a first example where Aristotle himself recognises that an inquiry depends importantly on *analogies* that enable connections to be drawn across genera, but *ipso facto* do not meet the requirements that he laid down for investigations *of* genera.

Then a second case takes us to the heart of the area of inquiry to which Aristotle devoted his most sustained, detailed and comprehensive researches, namely into animals, their properties and kinds. Some of the differences between the parts of animals that he considers are matters, he says, of degree, 'the more and the less'. Birds' wings, he says at *On the Parts of Animals* 644a19–22, differ by having longer or shorter feathers. But birds' feathers and the scales of fish differ more widely and correspond only 'by analogy', as do bone and fish-spine, nail and hoof, hand and claw (*History of Animals* 486b19–21). In most such cases the parts that are said to be analogically the same perform the same function, although Aristotle does not have a distinction equivalent to that between homology and analogy, between what is morphologically and genetically similar on the one hand versus what merely has the same function on the other.

In many of the instances Aristotle cites those functions are readily verifiable: hands and claws both serve to grasp things. But matters become more complicated when the 'by analogy' relationship serves as the articulating framework for the classification of animals as a whole. The two main groups of animals that Aristotle identifies are named 'blooded' and 'bloodless', the former including birds and fish as well as quadrupeds and humans, the latter consisting of four main kinds, which are named, in the conventional translations, 'cephalopods', 'crustacea', 'testacea' and 'insects'. Yet those four 'bloodless' animals have what is 'analogous to' blood. They have no heart, but they have what is analogous to it, and again no flesh but what is analogous to flesh.

The importance of this idea should not be underestimated since it provides Aristotle with a way of linking together the whole of the animal kingdom from humans to insects. Flesh is, for him, the main organ or medium of the most basic of the modes of perception, touch. The heart is the control centre of the animal and is, he believes, the first part to be differentiated as the embryo grows. Blood, meanwhile, serves, in his view, the basic function of nourishing the animal. So it is essential, one might say, for the bloodless creatures to have the analogues to these parts for them to function as animals.

But while in quite a number of cases Aristotle could reassure himself that there was indeed some part of an octopus, say, that serves the function of flesh, he is notably reticent about what exactly 'what is analogous to blood' covers. In such a case Aristotle does not discover an analogy so much as postulate one, with greater or less plausibility. In fact, as has been pointed out, in the case of 'blood' he may even underestimate the strength of his proposal, insofar as modern biology can confirm that many of the fluids that would not count as blood for Aristotle (for only red blood does) do indeed perform an analogous respiratory function.[26]

The tension between Aristotle's often brilliant perception of analogies in zoology and the restrictions seemingly imposed on their use by his theory of demonstration in the *Posterior Analytics* poses an interpretive crux. It is no good arguing that Aristotle changed his mind, that he either wrote the *Organon* before he had undertaken detailed zoological investigations (though in all probability his studies of animals continued throughout his life), or alternatively that the *Organon* came to reject or qualify the concepts and methods used in the zoological treatises. That will not do, as already in the *Organon* he not only gives botanical illustrations, but discusses the 'sameness by analogy' relationship with a standard zoological example at *Posterior Analytics* 98a20–2. At that point he complains that there is no

[26] As Peck remarked (1937: note to *PA* 645b9) and cf. Lloyd (1996b: 154n).

common name to cover the pounce of an octopus, fish-bone and bone,
though we should note that the lack of a name proved no deterrent when
he came to classify the bloodless animals, since in each case he either had
to coin the name of the class or adapt an existing Greek term. His word
for 'bloodless' itself (*anaimon*) had not been used of that main subdivision
of animals before.

His concern to give causal explanations is as strong in his zoology as it
is anywhere in his inquiry concerning nature. Thus far the ideals of the
Posterior Analytics certainly can be said to remain just that, his ideal. But
it is not just the case that those ideals are more difficult to apply to a
subject-matter as complex as zoology, but also that in certain respects at
least Aristotle realised that. The discussion of definition and of demonstration that is appropriate to animals departs from the model supplied by
such a discipline as geometry, precisely insofar as zoology depends on the
recognition of sameness by analogy. That indeed provides him, as I noted,
with the link that unites the whole of the animal kingdom.

The question that then arises, of course, is when exactly what are presented as analogous functions in different animals are indeed so. What
is analogous to blood in the bloodless animals proves to be a positive
example. But when Aristotle identifies the *mutis* of an octopus as its analogue to a heart (*On the Parts of Animals* 681b26–30), modern zoology
would say it performs rather the function of a liver. Aristotle is less articulate, we may say, on the modes of verification of his analogies than he is
on setting out a model to which explanations should in principle conform.
At the same time the methods of verification available to him to check
what precisely the octopus' *mutis* does were, of course, pretty limited. The
ability of analogies to generate conjectures to be explored here, as so often
elsewhere, outran the resources that could be brought to bear to test the
results of those explorations directly.

Aristotle's zoology is undoubtedly the most remarkable Greek example
of the use of systematic heuristic analogies in the study of nature, but it
is certainly not the only one. Theophrastus' extensive botanical works, the
History of Plants and the *Causes of Plants*, follow the Aristotelian model in
three respects and go beyond it in a fourth. First there is a recurrent preoccupation with the similarities and differences between plants and animals, to the point where he feels the need to issue a caveat, to the effect
that one should not expect a *complete* correspondence between them.[27]

---

[27] Theophrastus, *History of Plants* 1 1, 3–4. At 1 1, 5 he includes consideration of the analogies between
plants and animals among his general methods.

Secondly, he looks for a kind of plant that will serve as a model or paradigm for the rest of the plant kingdom, just as in Aristotle humans are used as the model by which other animals are judged, even the ideal to which in a sense they aspire.[28] Theophrastus finds this in trees which he explicitly takes as a standard for other plants (*History of Plants* I 1, 9–12). Thirdly, just as in Aristotle, he takes into account parts that are not exactly, but only analogously, the same across groups (e.g. I 1, 11). But then, fourthly, he is particularly concerned with a problem that did not surface so prominently in Aristotle's account of animals, namely whether the 'wild' or the 'domesticated' specimens of a species are more 'natural', concluding – from some points of view surprisingly – that in the case of trees it is the cultivated kind that is, on the grounds that it is only under cultivation that the kind can fulfil its full potential.[29]

As a coda to this section, let me turn back briefly to China once again, where there is, to be sure, no analogue in early times to Aristotle's detailed zoological investigations, nor to Theophastus' botanical ones.[30] Yet we find in the *Huainanzi*, for example, some brief remarks not just on how different groups of animals are to be correlated with the five phases, but also on such matters as the varying lengths of their period of gestation. In ch. 4, especially, we are told that animals that eat without chewing have eight bodily openings and lay eggs, while animals with nine bodily openings produce living young. Again having horns goes with having no upper incisors, while in the case of fat animals that have no horns, they have molars but no incisors. The overall concern of this section in the *Huainanzi* is with whether animals are predominantly yin or yang, but it is striking that while the correlations noted between the kind of teeth and horns would have occasioned some deductive arguments in Aristotle, the Chinese text is not interested in deduction so much as in correlation.

IV

Thus far I have been discussing the heuristic power of explicit or implicit analogies and comparisons, where such involve new suggestions, conjectures, hypotheses. But we should now open up the question of the relationships of similarity that are presupposed in the use of any generic term

---

[28] I discussed this in some detail in Lloyd (1983: 26–43), noting both instances where animals are thought of as deformed or maimed in comparison with humans, and also, conversely, where other animals are acknowledged to have, for example, superior sense-faculties to those of humans.

[29] See e.g. *History of Plants* II 1–4, and cf. Wardy (2005) on the Aristotelian olive in particular.

[30] The first detailed and systematic Chinese botanical treatise was the work of Li Shizhen in the sixteenth century, although it has some less systematic antecedents, see Métailié (forthcoming).

in any natural language. The concept I have just been discussing, namely 'animal', will serve as an excellent example, for it is one that figures importantly in just about every society whether or not the natural language it uses has a single term for it. This is certainly at the centre of both Greek and Chinese moral and religious thought as well as in their ideas about living beings as such – as I discussed in Lloyd (2012a). It has too a fundamental place in each of the divergent ontological regimes that the anthropologists have reported. So it is time to turn back to see what we can learn from ethnology about the boundaries between different kinds of living being.

To recapitulate the points of Descola's analysis (2013) that are relevant here, in totemism human groups are identified usually, though not exclusively, with particular kinds of animals, where similarities and continuities are posited in both respects, physicality and interiority. Naturalism firmly distinguishes animals on the interiority axis, for non-human ones do not have proper cultures, only humans do, though we and they are all made of the same material. Animism, by contrast, maintains continuity in interiority – other animals are persons, have souls, have social relations – but they differ from humans because of the bodies they possess. Analogism, finally, in Descola's view, distinguishes humans and animals in both interiority and physicality but sets up correspondences between them, as I illustrated previously by reference to the Chinese theory of the five phases, which proposes correlations right across the board from physical items through emotional and religious ones, to political institutions.

Our starting-point must be that 'animal' is in no sense a single given cross-cultural category. We may think, as may others, that in normal circumstances it is easy enough to recognise something as an animal. Indeed it is vital for hunters and pastoralists to have pretty detailed knowledge of animal kinds and their behaviours. Yet, as I noted before, even if we would like to take modern biology as authoritative, that does not provide definitive and unequivocal answers not just about the classes of animals, but also about what it is that distinguishes animals from plants and what marks the living out from the inanimate. To the problems within genetics and evolutionary theory we have to add those from ethology, where views on the intelligence that animals may display, their ability to communicate with one another and their social relations, have shifted dramatically in the last few decades. I shall be returning to those issues in Chapter 5.

It is important to register, even if it comes as no surprise, that in both the ancient societies that I have taken as the prime targets for my discussion there is widespread doubt and disagreement. As already noted, the Chinese sometimes correlated the main kinds of animals with the five phases. In the

Huainanzi 4: 16a9ff., the five groups are 'naked', 'feathered', 'hairy', 'scaly' and 'shelled' associated with Earth, Fire, Metal, Wood and Water respectively. The 'naked' (*ba*) animals are here identified with humans, though other ancient Chinese texts use analogous terms (*luo¹* and *luo²*) for comparatively hairless creatures, illustrated by tigers and leopards. *Huainanzi* here does not use an overarching term for 'animal' as such. The word often employed for non-human animals in general, namely *shou¹*, is here used for the hairy ones. Nor does it use the generic term *dongwu*, 'moving thing', which is the modern term for 'animal', though that is found in one early text, the *Zhouli* (2.1: 20.4ff., cf. Sterckx 2002: 15–21 at 19 and n. 25). Meanwhile in the *Erya* (13–19)[31] we find a different five-fold classification, *chong* ('insects' but the term can be used of many other creatures), *yu* (fish), *niao* (birds), *shou¹* ('beasts', here wild ones) and *chu* (domesticated animals, themselves divided elsewhere into five groups, chicken, sheep, oxen, dogs and pigs – where *yang* for sheep covers goats as well).

Neither the term for animal in general, nor the identification of the main groupings, is stable. Indeed the first complication in that regard comes with the extensive Chinese interest in metamorphoses (which caused problems for Aristotle as well, cf. Lloyd 1996b: ch. 5). Various classical texts speak not just of the metamorphoses of insects, but also, for example, of swallows and sparrows turning into clams (*Huainanzi* 4: 9b3f.) or of hawks changing into pigeons (5: 2b).[32] It is tempting to evaluate these according to how they make sense in our terms, and this has occasioned a good deal of rationalising interpretation (e.g. Major 1993: 228ff. suggesting the hawks and pigeons example may be to do with the annual migrations of the two species). But that may often be to miss the point. When *Zhuangzi* (18: 47.45, cf. *Liezi* 1: 2.19–3.1) has certain plants producing panthers and panthers producing horses and horses humans, his interests may be miles away from 'zoology' or 'ecology'. The chapter may be more concerned to problematise who exactly anyone is, to shake our confidence that we can unequivocally identify stable individuals around us, even including ourselves. This was the text after all that elsewhere (2: 7.93ff.) asked whether Zhuangzi, having just woken up, had dreamed he was a butterfly, or whether this was now a butterfly dreaming it was Zhuangzi.

When we come to a text such as *Xunzi* (9: 16a) which sets out a hierarchy of beings, it is clear that its chief concern is with what distinguishes human

---

[31] The *Erya* is not so much a dictionary as a compendium explaining certain terms: it is thought to date from the third century BCE.

[32] The first chapter of *Liezi* (which may date mostly from the third or fourth century CE) is a rich mine of other examples of metamorphoses, ably discussed by Sterckx (2002: ch. 6).

beings from everything else. After water and fire that are said to have qi^1 but not life ($sheng^1$), we have first 'grasses and trees' (cao, mu) that have life but no awareness, and then 'birds and beasts' (qin, $shou^1$) standing in for animals in general, who have awareness in addition. Top of the list come humans, where we certainly leave anything we might want to call 'biology' behind, for their identifying characteristic is yi^1, morality.

The Greeks regularly used $z\bar{o}on$ for animal in general (including humans) but the root of that term, the verb $z\bar{e}n$, means to live and applies to plants as well, as indeed sometimes $z\bar{o}on$ also does (Plato, *Timaeus* 77bc). Yet exactly what distinguishes plants from animals was a point on which theorists disagreed. Can plants perceive? Plato answered yes, but in Aristotle perception is a characteristic of animals, not of plants. Theophrastus denied characters ($\bar{e}th\bar{e}$) and actions (*praxeis*) to plants, but spoke of their ways of life (*bioi*) (*History of Plants* 1 1) and described the associations between them in terms of their friendships or kinships, even tentatively suggesting that plants may resemble animals in that respect (*Causes of Plants* 11 17, 5).

Yet Aristotle, great zoologist that he is, is less dogmatic on this topic than is generally assumed. It is true that there are innumerable passages in which he states, in apparently categorical terms, that the defining property of animals is perception. Yet on two occasions he hesitates, and with good reason. At *History of Animals* 588b4–589a2 he remarks that 'nature moves from the non-living to animals little by little', and further that there is a continuity between plants and animals. Again in the *Parts of Animals* 681a12–20 he says that 'nature moves continuously from lifeless things to the animals through things that are alive but not animals'. He is there immersed in a discussion of what to say about a number of problematic species, sea-squirts, sponges, sea-anemones, sea-lungs (jellyfish), the pinna and the razor-shell. The sea-anemones, for instance, 'dualise' between a plant and an animal: they do not belong to the group he calls Testacea but fall outside the main classes, having some of the properties of animals (they can live detached from the rocks on which they are found, and they appear to perceive what comes up against them) but also some of those of plants (they quickly attach themselves and they do not excrete).

The most surprising discussion relates to the jellyfish, which differ from the sponges in that they are detached, rather than anchored to the seabed, but 'they have no perception, but live like plants that are detached'. The lessons of this text are considerable since it implies that – contrary to those generalisations I mentioned – perception is not always what distinguishes plants from animals. These creatures, the jellyfish, are still included among the animals, since they can live detached, unlike plants (though there are complications on that side of the contrast as well, as some plants seem to be exceptions to that rule). So instead of a crisp unequivocal single criterion that points to perception as the distinguishing mark of animals we have to note that he concedes that in some problematic cases it is the ability to live detached that serves that function.

The conclusion we should draw is not that, for Aristotle, 'animal' is equivocal, nor that it fails to provide a field of study in which causal connections can be sought and found. But what it is to be an animal is to be answered by a disjunctive definition in which plural criteria are involved and in practice, in the field as it were, the application of those criteria can be problematic. The lesson is that in certain contexts even Aristotle, the arch-stickler for univocity, has to, and does, qualify the applicability of his ideal in the face of the complexities of the phenomena.

Of course Aristotle does not draw any conclusions to the effect that the phenomena are, as I put it, multidimensional. Nor does he have a notion that is equivalent to what I call 'semantic stretch'.[33] Yet he surely recognises that the viability of the general terms that natural language presents us with always depends precisely on the evaluation of the similarities and differences they presuppose. His presupposition was that there are indeed genera and species that clearly defined terms should correctly represent. The difficulty of accepting that ideal across the board is the problem that my next study takes up. For now I would conclude that the heuristic use of analogy shows both its power and its limitations: there can be no foolproof rule for getting the answers right, for sifting out the misleading similarities and differences from those that are fit for purpose, where the purposes themselves will reflect the interests and the agenda of those raising the issues in the first place. But we can see that the quality of our understanding depends very much on our using our best judgement in that regard even though not, I argue, in any expectation that we can somehow immunise our procedures against error.

[33] He does, however, speak of some terms that apply *pros hen* rather than univocally (*kath' hen*), in what is generally called his theory of 'focal meaning'. The canonical example of this is the term 'healthy', applied primarily to health itself, but derivatively of signs of health (a 'healthy' complexion) or to what promotes or preserves health (a healthy diet or climate). That certainly picks out what I call semantic stretch, but his assumption is that this is a feature of certain exceptional terms, rather than (as I claim for semantic stretch) one that potentially permeates all language use. (cf. Lloyd 1996b: ch. 7).

CHAPTER 5

Ontologies revisited

One theme I have developed in earlier chapters is that apprehending similarities and differences is basic to cognition. All natural languages provide their users with a rich haul of general terms, and the genera and species in question evidently depend on an apprehension of the similarities between their respective members. Given that this is a basic feature of language, we have no need to speculate that it has a specific origin in human social groupings (though that is not to deny the huge importance of social experience in human reasoning in general, as has been argued by Humphrey 1976, 1992, Byrne and Whiten 1988, Dupré 2002 among others). Durkheim and Mauss overdid it when they claimed that classification itself not only reflects social organisation but is indeed essentially social, as when they asserted that 'the first logical categories were social categories; the first classes of things were classes of men' (Durkheim and Mauss 1963 [1903]: 82). That was a thesis that was open to both logical and empirical objections as was set out in detail by their translator Rodney Needham (1963: xi–xxxix).

Thus it is somewhat of an exaggeration to suggest that classification is inherently a social act, essentially focusing on social groupings, rather than a basic and entirely general cognitive activity, and the linguistic evidence from terms for 'genus', 'kind', 'species' in different languages is mixed. The anthropologist Scott Atran, whose work on indigenous classifications of animals I shall be considering shortly, only managed to elicit the claimed underlying 'natural' classification among the Itza Maya when he bypassed their indigenous groupings and asked which creatures are 'companions' (*et'ok*) to which. In classical Greek the primary connotation of the term *genos* (from which our own 'genus' is ultimately derived) is indeed 'family' or 'tribe'. But the principal ancient Greek word used for sub-groups or species, namely *eidos*, has 'form' or 'appearance' as its primary connotation.[1] One

---

[1] Aristotle graded the various ways in which some items may be one and the same as others, that is in number (Socrates is the same individual as the son of Sophroniscus), in *eidos* (Socrates and Callias are both humans), in *genos* (humans and horses are both animals) and finally, as we saw in Chapter 4, 'by analogy'.

of the classical Chinese terms for 'kind', namely *zhong*, refers in the first instance to what is sown, in other words to seeds. However, the basic logical point, that classification cannot but depend on the grasp of similarities, is confirmed by the principal Chinese word for categories, namely *lei*, which we have met several times already, for its core use is to refer to the groups or groupings of items of different sorts united by associations, resonances or resemblances. It comes in modern times to be used verbally for 'to resemble' and adjectivally to express the notion of 'similar'.

It is still commonly assumed both that there *are* natural kinds and that they are, on the whole, adequately represented in the languages we use, though I have thrown doubt on both assumptions,[2] and certainly the kinds actually picked out by different natural languages exhibit considerable diversity. But as is also universally acknowledged, similarities may be misleading. Some philosophies, some religions, some areas of science, develop a strong theoretical contrast between appearance and reality, but, even without that, everyone realises that things may not be as they seem. In other words, we may be taken in by a superficial or an imagined resemblance.

So the recurrent problem is: which similarities, which differences, are to be trusted? The notion that there is a single determinate reality out there to which appeal can be made to validate the correct similarities and confute the imposters, has been found to run into all sorts of difficulties. It would be nice to believe that the science of the day delivers reliable answers to such a question across the board, even though there are many areas of human experience that science does not cover. But evidently the science of the day changes, has changed and will continue to do so. Today's scientists include, no doubt, some of the best ones who have ever lived, but they are not exactly infallible, even though they can successfully diagnose and avoid many particular mistakes that their predecessors made. Individuals, whether specialists or just lay persons, and whole groups, disagree fundamentally about what there is, in ways that, as the anthropologists have shown, affect how they live, their relations with others, their ways of being in their world.

The difficult task this chapter sets itself is, then, to examine the objective bases for the similarities, images, models and analogies we commonly rely on. The chief problem is easily expressed. The idea that there is an external reality out there to which access is possible unmediated by theories and preconceptions is, as I have said, a chimera. There can be no

---

[2] Hacking engaged in a devastating critique of 'natural kinds' in Hacking (2007): cf. Khalidi (2013).

such thing as a description of the phenomena that is entirely neutral in the sense of theory-free. As for the apprehension of similarities of which I have just spoken, everything will depend on which ones are taken to be relevant and by what criteria, and there is, again, no neutral way of deciding that, for we may always ask, relevant to whom, and for what purposes?

On the other hand, few would want to deny that over large areas of what we call cosmology, physics, chemistry, biology, considerable advances in understanding have been made and surely more will be. So how do we reconcile the competing claims of relativists and universalists in this area? Some of the former will protest that every set of answers reflects certain assumptions that can be challenged and none can claim universal validity. Some of the latter will insist that the natural characters and properties of things, their essences, even, are there to be discovered.

Let me explain the tactics of my discussion. I shall begin with some of those areas of natural science where claims for progress in knowledge seem strongest, in particular in the understanding of the structure of the universe and of some of its components, and especially of animals, plants and diseases. That will be a preliminary to confronting the apparently fundamental clashes between different ontologies as revealed both by the historical record and by ethnography where we must return to the problems of translating and judging between them that, as I mentioned before, stem principally from recent anthropology. An analysis of their variety, including in particular the different ways in which they draw on analogies, will lead me to reject on the one hand the radical sceptical position according to which there is, after all, no mind-independent reality, but also on the other the assumption that the ontological issues can be resolved in favour of a unique definitive answer. The notion of the multidimensionality of reality, I suggest, is the best way to do justice to pluralism without licensing the conclusion that just anything goes.

Natural science has, over the years, delivered a mass of what we normally accept as robust results in astrophysics, through geophysics and chemistry to all the areas covered by biology, from anatomy, physiology, zoology, botany to genetics and medicine. While the discovery that the planets differ in their apparent movements from the other stars is ancient, the identification of galaxies, the exploration of the structure of our galaxy, and the classification of different types of celestial objects, red giants, white dwarfs and the rest, are of course comparatively recent. There are plenty of questions that remain unanswered, about what happened in the first microseconds after the Big Bang, about dark energy and anti-matter, about the actual constitution of the fundamental particles of which everything is made, about the forms of life that other solar systems might sustain, even about hidden dimensions of space and time. But we think we have more or less clear ideas about the kinds of methods that will have to be used to resolve them, even if not all of them are currently within our grasp, and in some cases (string theory would be one example, cf. Smolin 2006) whether we are on the right track remains controversial. Indeed many will say that merely human intelligence will not be up to the task, even though that is the highest type of intelligence of which we are aware.

In most domains of natural science, however, we, in the twenty-first century, can claim to know a good deal more about many aspects of the phenomena we are faced with than any of our predecessors wherever in the world they lived. Our understanding of animals has sometimes been thought to be an exception to that, insofar as there are powerful advocates of a view that the main groups of animals are, and have always been, correctly identified by humans everywhere. Everyone has to concede that on the surface the classifications of animals adopted by different human groups differ widely, reflecting very different interests, including theories about how animals reproduce and move, the extent to which they can be domesticated, and especially about which ones should provide food for humans. But Berlin, Breedlove and Raven (1973) argued that there are some five or six general, if not universal, ethno-biological categories that underpin and are present in such taxonomies worldwide. These categories form a hierarchy, starting from a Unique Beginner, through Life Form, Generic and Specific, down to Varietal. The different taxonomic levels are not all necessarily labelled in any given natural language (we have noted that initially Chinese had no label for 'animal' as such). Again the genera and species that are picked out by a given human population differ to some extent, where local ecological variations have an important part to play. But species will always be subsumed under genera which in turn fall under Life Form – or so the argument goes.

In several important publications (1990, 1995, 1998) Scott Atran takes the argument a step further. Undertaking investigations on the one hand on the Itza' Maya in central Mexico and on the other on American undergraduates, he found basic similarities in the answers to questions about which kinds of animals 'go with' which or are 'companions' to which. Moreover those answers exhibit impressive correspondences to the findings of modern zoological taxonomy. Those points, he argued, provide grounds for a claim for a more or less universal 'common-sense' classification of animals across all human populations.[3]

Now it would be nice to believe that all humans are naturally equipped to identify accurately the genera, species and varieties of animals – and why, one might ask, would that not extend also to plants, minerals, diseases, indeed all those natural kinds that are commonly assumed? A case can be made that non-human animals too derive an evolutionary advantage from being able to distinguish correctly the various kinds of predators and of prey by whom they are surrounded: experience must teach them that quite quickly – although whether other animals reason to their conclusions or the extent to which they do was controversial already in Greek antiquity (Sorabji 1993, Osborne 2007, Lloyd 2012a: ch. 1) and remains highly contested today (e.g. Griffin 1984, 1992, Dupré 2002, Daston and Mitman 2005). But the distinctions we and the other animals need for bare survival purposes do not extend beyond the comparatively large creatures that are, or have in our evolutionary past been, familiar in our immediate environment. One considerable objection to the more general claim, if we have this natural ability to get animal groups right, is to explain how it comes about that the explicit classifications we actually encounter, in all their variety, ever conflict with what zoological taxonomy suggests. Atran protests that this happens only rarely:[4] but why it should ever occur is (on this hypothesis) mysterious.

But far more important for our purposes here, there is no agreement, among taxonomists themselves, about the groupings formed by the principal kingdoms of the eukaryotes.[5] Partly this is due to contingent reasons, the gaps in the fossil record. But partly also for fundamental ones, namely that in many cases the boundaries themselves appear to be indeterminate. Quite what status to assign to hybrids, sports and mutants is often deeply problematic. This itself is part of an even more radical difficulty, of determining what zoological species are. After Darwin had demolished the notion of their eternity, that was a question raised in the sharpest terms

---

[3] I discussed Atran's views, including certain apparent shifts in his position in Lloyd (2007a: ch. 3). It is particularly striking that in some of their more recent studies he and his colleagues recognise the impoverished knowledge of animals and plants among many urbanised Westerners. They call this the devolution of knowledge, but it is rather a degradation of it (see Ross 2002, Ross, Medin, Coley and Atran 2003 and Atran, Medin and Ross 2004).

[4] See Atran (1990: 268). The problems posed by whales and bats are, he holds, exceptional.

[5] The eukaryotes include not just animals, plants and fungi but also a vast proliferation of microorganisms, rhizaria, excavata, chromalveolata and the rest. In a fast-moving field I outlined what was then current thinking on the topic in Lloyd (2007a: ch. 3).

by Mayr and his colleagues (1957) and never satisfactorily answered, as the ongoing disputes between, for example, Ghiselin (1974), Dupré (1993, 2001), Hull (2001) and their adherents and opponents so clearly show. We may command rough and ready notions adequate for ordinary purposes, but while we seem not to be able to do without some notion of species, we are rather in a position like that of Augustine facing the problem of saying what time is,[6] in that we find it difficult to determine precisely what our notion covers. Essentialist assumptions, here and elsewhere, prove to be anything but securely founded, even though developmental psychologists have shown how even very young children tend to adopt them (Carey 1985, Keil 1989, Carey and Spelke 1994, Carey 2009).

Advances in the study of every kind of living thing, especially those that have been made in the last four or five decades, have brought to light innumerable features that were quite unsuspected in previous generations. These were discoveries, not inventions, even though the methods used to reveal them had indeed to be invented. At least most would agree that genes existed before they were identified as such. Many of the groupings that have commonly been perceived by human populations across the world remain useful: thus far we may agree with the thrust of Atran's argument. Our ancestors in the Pleistocene needed basic knowledge of the predators and prey in their environment which indeed they had to recognise immediately. For that they had to use what Gigerenzer and others have dubbed 'fast and frugal' reasoning,[7] with no time to worry about the finer points of classification, about which kinds formed higher genera and which did not. Where plants were concerned, again, the edible had to be distinguished from the inedible, those with curative properties from poisonous ones, even though the same plant could and often did span both those categories, with medicinal properties in small doses, lethal ones in larger. Recognition of the character and causes of diseases, and not just those that traditional herbal remedies could alleviate, was much slower in coming but now far surpasses what was understood before the nineteenth century.

All of that can be chalked up as notable successes in the search for objective knowledge. We have firmer grounds for the groupings we now use, and can distinguish similarities and differences of different types, some merely superficial, others reflecting the underlying biology. Yet what

---

[6] Augustine famously proclaimed that he understood time until he was asked to say what exactly it was: 'Quid est ergo tempus? Si nemo ex me quaerat, scio; si quaerenti explicare velim, nescio.' (What then is time? If no one asks me, I know: but if I want to explain what it is to a questioner, I don't.) *Confessions* XI ch. 14.

[7] Gigerenzer and Goldstein (1996), Gigerenzer and Todd (1999), cf. Kahneman (2011).

biological research reveals is also the flexibilities and plasticity of genes, exemplified most startlingly, perhaps, by the mutations that pathogens undergo. That is one reason why cancer and AIDS have proved so difficult to cure. Both present not determinate, but constantly shifting targets for treatment. So we need to be wary of essentialist assumptions not just about animals, but about the basic subject-matter with which all the biological sciences have to deal. At a superficial level, as we said, the main species and genera of animals, plants, diseases may look stable enough. Their deeper analysis soon reveals the fluidity and plasticity in the basic building blocks of all organic matter.[8] What used to be kept firmly separated in the two categories of nature and nurture turn out to be not distinct, well-defined substances, but rather boundary-crossing interactive processes.

Thus far I have been commenting largely on the achievements of science. But it does not have a monopoly to the answer we should give to the question of what there is. I shall be dealing with feelings and morality later, but both philosophy and religion have, in the past, laid claims to deliver at least elements of the answer, and, according to some, the most important ones. The methods, or at least the tactics they have relied on to justify those claims, differ widely from those of the sciences, and one immediate problem here again is the total lack of any consensus about the conclusions to be drawn. The cynic would argue that the pronouncements of both philosophy and religion stem exclusively from ideological considerations, so that the only comments we can make relate to sociological factors, to the power struggles that are played out by those who have purported to have privileged access to the truth.

For the purposes of my explorations of ontological issues here we may leave most of those controversies to one side. However, one major ontological distinction, to be found already in ancient philosophy, certainly is relevant to my study. I refer to the broad contrast between two views about what is basic in reality, one that answers that in terms of substances, the second in terms of processes.[9]

Of course the most articulate ancient spokesman of the substance-based view was Aristotle, while powerful expressions of a process-based ontology are to be found in Chinese thought. Yet as I shall go on to point out, it

---

[8] The literature on the subject is by now immense, but see especially Keller (2000), Avital and Jablonka (2000) and Jablonka and Lamb (2014).

[9] We may recall Quine's discussion of the possible referents of 'gavagai' in his hypothetical ethnographic example, where we can see that he distinguished, among other things, an answer in terms of events from one in terms of objects or substances (cf. above, p. 14). But his example reflects the more general problem of the gap that opens up between a process-based and a substance-based understanding of what there is. In what follows I recapitulate the arguments of Lloyd (2014).

would be absurd to represent all of Greek philosophy as wedded to the priority of substances or indeed all of Chinese philosophy as committed to a process-based view. First, however, let me outline Aristotle's own position and explain some of the complexities it incorporates.

In the *Categories* he distinguishes a number of categories, substances, qualities, quantities, relations and so on (we have, in fact, rather different, more or less inclusive lists, in different works, of the fundamental categories he recognises). These all represent different ways in which something can be said to be, for he believes it to be important to distinguish the different answers that can be given to that question. Red, for example, is a colour, and colour is a quality: but qualities are not to be confused with substances (a point he uses to criticise Plato's theory of Forms: some of Plato's Forms relate to qualities, the good or the beautiful, others to substances, animal, human). But all the other categories depend on substance in a sense he explains in admittedly rather opaque terms. Those other categories all exist 'in' a subject and that means that they cannot exist independently or separately from what they are 'in'.[10] Qualities cannot exist independently of substances to qualify (another point he makes against Plato).

But how can a similar argument not apply also to substances? They can exist independently of this or that particular quality. But a totally quality-less substance is as inconceivable (we would say) as a quality that is not a quality of some substance. It has been argued that Aristotle's point is rather that the dependence of the other categories on substances is a matter of the need to refer, eventually, to substance when giving an account of what they are – where such a dependence relationship is not true of substances themselves. But however we explain Aristotle's view on that, it is certainly the case that he *asserts* that if the primary substances (individuals) did not exist, it would be impossible for any of the other things to exist (*Categories* 2b5–6), a claim that has no counterpart in his account of quality, quantity, relation and the rest.

But then the next complication is Aristotle's claim, in *Metaphysics*, book Z, 1040b5–10, that many of the items that he says were commonly thought to be substances are rather just potentialities, *dunameis*. He specifies the parts of animals and the simple bodies (he names earth, fire and air, but

---

[10] Aristotle, *Categories* 1a20–b9. The exact interpretation of this passage is disputed, but that does not affect the main point I draw attention to, namely Aristotle's claim that substances are basic. Indeed in this work the primary substances are individuals, while the species and genera they form are 'secondary' substances, dependent for their existence on the individual primary substances that constitute them. If there were no individual humans, the species human would not exist. (Since, for him, the cosmos is eternal, he is not concerned with extinction events.)

we should also include the other simple body, water). The parts of animals do not exist independently of the living animal of which they are parts. A dead hand is a hand in name alone. As for the simple bodies, they are not substances unless they are 'concocted', that is elaborated or worked up into more complex entities. It turns out that on this rather restrictive view it is humans and members of other kinds of living beings that are the paradigmatic substances (a view that has evident similarities to, indeed direct connections with, the common-sense view of animals that Atran finds as a more or less universal human assumption[11]). Artefacts which depend on human craftsmen to make them turn out to be excluded, at least on the strict criteria with which Aristotle is working in this particular text.

Aristotle's metaphysics exemplifies how an ontology that privileges substances can be brought to bear to account for change, movement and indeed process themselves. Change is analysed as taking place between contrarieties of different sorts. Natural motion, for instance, is parsed in terms of the natural tendencies of the simple bodies, earth and water to move 'downwards' (to the centre of the earth, construed as the centre of the universe[12]) and fire and air to move 'upwards' to the periphery. Each of the simple bodies is characterised by a pair of contrary qualities. 'Water' which is cold and wet turns into 'air' which is hot and wet by the application of heat. But while the qualities of things, and their potentialities, find their place in his theories, the actualities in question are prior, in his view, both ontologically and logically. If we ask what primarily can be said to be, Aristotle's answer will be substances.

Aristotle's ontology became the default assumption of much later Western metaphysics. But while it passed for many people in the West as common sense, it was certainly not accepted by everyone, not even by all his fellow ancient Greeks. Before him, in the fifth century BCE, the Presocratic philosopher Heraclitus had proclaimed that the *kosmos* (world-order) is an 'everliving fire, kindled in measures and extinguished in measures' (Fr. 30) and indeed that everything is in constant flux. In a striking phrase that is attributed to him, you cannot step into the same river twice.[13] Again among Aristotle's successors his pupil and colleague Theophrastus raised a

---

[11] In his 1990 Atran draws on Aristotle extensively and explicitly in proposing his 'common-sense' view of animal kinds.

[12] In *On the Heavens* II chs. 13–14 Aristotle adduces both abstract and empirical arguments for his view that the earth is spherical and at rest at the centre of the universe. The relative weight and lightness of the four simple bodies are discussed in, for example, *On the Heavens* IV ch. 4.

[13] Heraclitus Fr. 91 and cf. Fr. 12.

fundamental problem about one of the simple bodies, namely fire, which unlike the other three cannot exist without a substratum (fuel). Fire is indeed a kind of movement.[14] Later, both the main Hellenistic positive philosophies disagreed with Aristotle. The Epicureans reverted to the view of Leucippus and Democritus that all that exists is atoms and the void, and the Stoics, who agreed with Aristotle in being teleologists, explained physical change in terms of their two fundamental principles one active and the other passive. At the same time the basic, apparently insoluble, controversies in cosmology and indeed every aspect of philosophical speculation led the Pyrrhonist sceptics to reject both reason and perception as reliable criteria. Instead they advocated suspension of judgement on all questions to do with hidden causes and underlying reality.[15]

I have rehearsed these well-known disputes in Greek ontology to point out that a substance-based ontology was not then (and to be sure still is not) a foregone conclusion, and to show further how mistaken it would be to claim that such an ontology was somehow determined by some circumstances of the situation in which Greek philosophy developed. Some have seen Aristotle's categories and substance-based ontologies as a whole as reflecting features of the Greek language, perhaps features it shares with other Indo-European languages more generally. Others have pointed to political circumstances, or geographical or climatological ones. But all such speculations face a major difficulty, namely the disagreement, among the Greeks themselves, about whether Aristotle was right, and further, about just what analysis to give of fundamental reality.[16]

Conversely the Chinese, who certainly bear witness to the attractions of a process-based ontology, cannot be said to have been led to such views by some feature of the natural language they used. It is true that the dominant cosmological doctrine, from Han times onwards, was based on the roles of the *wu xing*, the five phases, linked in two cycles, one of mutual conquest, the other of mutual production. In the former, Water overcomes Fire, which overcomes Metal, which overcomes Wood, which

---

[14] Theophrastus *On Fire* iii.

[15] Long and Sedley (1987) provides the best introductory source-book to the main philosophical sects of the Hellenistic period.

[16] That is not to say that political factors are not relevant to the development of Greek philosophy in general, and I shall deal with linguistic ones in the Supplementary Note at the end of this chapter. But the argument in the case of politics would not be that a particular political regime influenced the development of a particular physics or cosmology, so much as that political pluralism and debate contributed to a pluralism in such theories – and indeed philosophical pluralism probably had a feedback effect on the pluralism of political regimes by way of the variety of political systems it identified. I discuss the exceptional circumstances that contributed to the development of an ideal of strict demonstration in Greece briefly in Chapter 6.

overcomes Earth, which overcomes Water, to begin the whole cycle again.
In the latter, Wood produces Fire, which produces Earth, which produces
Metal, which produces Water, which produces Wood, again to restart the
cycle.[17] Although starting with the Jesuits when they entered China in the
sixteenth century, Westerners have repeatedly taken this to be a Chinese
element theory,[18] for the Chinese themselves the five are not substances, so
much as, precisely, phases. An early text makes this quite clear. In the *Hong
Fan* (part of the *Shang Shu* that may be dated to the third century BCE) we
read: 'Water means (*yue*) soaking downwards, Fire means flaming upwards,
Wood means bending and straightening, Metal means conforming and
changing, Earth means accepting seed and giving crops.'[19]

Yet once again very different pronouncements on the question of what is
can be found in other Chinese texts, which illustrate how mistaken it would
be to attempt to generalise about *the* Chinese view of what there is, let alone
about any such view to which some feature of their language committed
them. The *qiwulun* chapter (2) of the *Zhuangzi* especially engages in a
radical critique both of assertions and of denials of reality. This it does
both by a graphic image and by abstract analysis. You cannot assert 'it is',
nor 'it is not'. What one person deems to be so, another denies: the sage
relies on viewpoints – perspectives, we might say – but without a categorical
commitment to them. The chapter ends with the famous parable of the
butterfly that I mentioned before (p. 85). Zhuangzi wakes having dreamt
he was a butterfly. But was this Zhuangzi who wakes from a dream, or a
butterfly who now dreams it is Zhuangzi? Zhuangzi's concern, to be sure,
is not with ontology, but with how to live. But his attack on that question
evidently has implications for the answer to be given to what is – and that
answer is miles away from the speculations of cosmologists who used the
five phases to set up correlations across the whole range of the phenomena
of experience.

---

[17] Both cycles are found in the *Huainanzi* 4, cf. Major (1993: 186ff.). The gradual development of
five-phase theory, which may have originated as an account of dynastic change, is described in
Lloyd and Sivin (2002: Appendix 253ff.). It is worth noticing how the 'overcoming' in the conquest
cycle (*sheng*[2] in the fourth tone) and the 'producing' in the production cycle (*sheng*[1] in the first
tone) exhibit remarkable semantic stretch.

[18] The Jesuits themselves still adhered to a version of Aristotle's four-element theory, based on earth,
water, air and fire. So for them the Chinese five phases were just a botched job at such an
element theory, mistakenly omitting air and including Wood and Metal, which Aristotle would
have considered homogeneous compounds, not elements.

[19] This text in the *Hong Fan* (*Shangshu*, ch. 32) is discussed by Graham (1989: 326), and cf. Nylan
(2001: 239–41), Lloyd and Sivin (2002: 259–60). Of course water is also what you drink, and I shall
be mentioning later a further complication in Chinese views on the subject of water, namely when
its chief characteristic is said to be 'purity' (see below, p. 112).

This lengthy excursus into some Greek and Chinese views serves first, I trust, to show how in both these ancient societies very different positions were adopted on the question of what is basic in our experience of the world, and then to raise the issues of assessing them and translating between them. Of course much of what passed as sound detailed knowledge in ancient texts has been overtaken and superseded by subsequent investigations. Yet, as I pointed out before, evaluating ontologies is not a matter of assigning a simple true or false verdict to a well-formed proposition or even to a set of them. Certainly Aristotle and the *Huainanzi* do commit themselves to particular theories and explanations. For Aristotle the earth is spherical, for *Huainanzi* it is flat. Flat-earthers are now a diminishing cohort: but we should not forget that the horizon seems to present itself as a straight line (a point that Aristotle had to counter to maintain his spherical earth[20]).

More importantly, most ancient ontologies form a complex nexus of positions, cosmological, physical, biological, and also moral and political, that elude straightforward falsification[21]. That does not mean that they are hopelessly vague, let alone that they are beyond our understanding. We can certainly arrive at a provisional grasp both of their contents and of the considerations that weighed with their authors when they proposed them, and we can make our provisional judgements about the strengths and weaknesses of each.

If we confront the issue between a substance-based and a process-based ontology in particular, we should take stock of how both capture different aspects or dimensions of experience. The substance-based view, though not necessarily in its purest Aristotelian form, insists, perfectly reasonably, that the medium-sized physical objects in our local environment, both the animals and plants and the artefacts that surround us, enjoy a certain stability of existence. They are subject to change, for sure, but that does not mean that the table we try to move or paint disintegrates before we can do the moving or the painting. Mostly those changes occur at the microscopic level where modern physics would indeed endorse something closer to a Heraclitean flux or to Chinese constant interactive processes.[22]

---

[20] In *On the Heavens* 294a1–7 he says that those who hold that the earth is flat refer to the appearance of the sun when it rises or sets. Where it is cut off by the horizon, the line is straight. But if the earth were spherical, that line would be curved. But to that he counters that they ignore the distance of the sun (though that, we should say, is irrelevant) and the size of the earth (which is, on the contrary, the key point).

[21] This was a point urged against such views by those, such as Popper, who insisted on falsifiability as a test of scientificity.

[22] Both general relativity and quantum mechanics may be said to make processes prior to states. In the wake not just of the development of modern physics, but also of such classic studies as

That occasioned a good deal of not very fruitful modern philosophical discussion as to which was the 'real' table, the one the furniture dealer sells us or the one that atomic physics describes. But any attempt to settle for one answer *to the exclusion of* the other pays a heavy price, by simply dismissing the possibility that the other has anything to be said in its favour. If we are not obsessed by a misconceived ambition to arrive at a single definitive answer, we can have it both ways. The table both is a heap of constantly moving molecules and has the approximately stable properties we perceive. 'Reality' is multidimensional, in this case because the accounts we can give vary according to the level of analysis we attempt. We can stop at the phenomenal level, where the table appears solid enough, or we can proceed to finer and finer descriptions of its molecular, atomic and subatomic constituents.[23]

But even if I can claim that such a view has certain advantages in the process/substance case, what about the far more complex, but admittedly looser, schemata that the anthropologists have reported? It is time to bring back into the picture Descola's four-fold classification, of animism, totemism, analogism and naturalism, and Viveiros de Castro's perspectivism. Here we are dealing not with explicit theories, backed up with more or less sophisticated philosophical arguments, both physical and epistemological. Rather, we are dealing with reports of very diverse reactions to experience, with ways of being in the world and living social lives, with values and morality, where those reactions carry implications concerning the presuppositions made about how humans relate to other things in the world, and indeed about that world itself. Evidently there are two aspects to this problem, one a matter of intellectual understanding, the other one of assessing the consequences for how one should live. But the latter presupposes a positive answer to the former, and I shall accordingly concentrate on it here, picking up the issues of translation and intelligibility I broached in Chapter 1.

those of Bergson (1911 [1907]) and Whitehead (1978 [1929]: part II, ch. 10 especially) quite a few contemporary physicists and philosophers of science have advocated a process-based rather than an entity-based account of reality, among them notably Prigogine and Stengers (Prigogine 1980, Prigogine and Stengers 1997, Stengers 2010). Smolin (2000) included a chapter (4) that was entitled 'The Universe is made of processes, not things'. In that he stated (52) that 'there are not really two categories of things in the world: objects and processes. There are only relatively fast processes and relatively slow processes' – a view strangely reminiscent of the theory of perception Plato discussed in the *Theaetetus* 156a–157c, which does away with stable objects and postulates an interaction between faster movements and slower ones.

23 We should also allow that 'table' has semantic stretch on this score, even before we come to tables of opposites, logarithmic tables, water tables and the rest.

The diversity of the regimes in question certainly goes far beyond a simple contrast between a substance- and a process-based conception. In Viveiros de Castro's perspectivism, other beings, not just humans, are social creatures, and see things in the way they do because they have the bodies they have. Indigenous peoples see a jaguar drinking the blood of its prey. They are in no doubt about that. But the jaguar itself sees that blood as manioc beer. Jaguars go off and live in communities organised very much in the way in which human societies are, with moieties governing social relations, even with their own shamans. Every kind of living being apprehends experience in its own way, thanks to the body it has.

In Descola's account, perspectivism is subsumed under animism, but, as we noted, that is just one of four regimes defined in terms of the positions adopted first on interiority (feelings about self) and then on physicality (the bodies each being possesses). Animism, in this account, as we pointed out, presupposes continuity on the interiority axis, but discontinuity on the physicality one (beings are differentiated by their bodies). Totemism sees continuities on both axes, while analogism assumes discontinuities on both. Finally naturalism, the default ontology of modernity as he claims, assumes discontinuities on the interiority axis (humans alone possess culture) but continuities on the physicality one (we are all made of the same stuff).

These reports present a very different crux from the philosophical arguments we considered earlier. Are we to say that just one of them is correct, while the other three are mistaken, even seriously deluded? That is the view generally taken by naturalism in particular, which assumes it has a proprietary claim on saying how the world is. I have already criticised that opinion at length, first on the grounds of intellectual imperialism, secondly on the question of the concept of nature itself, in my account a cultural product, and to that extent culturally relative, and thirdly on the basis of the limits of the type of knowledge that naturalist science delivers.

But are the differences between these schemata such that it is strictly impossible to make any comparative judgements about them? Certainly there is no neutral vantage point from which that could begin, no discourse about them that is entirely theory-free. We may often have to admit to bafflement, as the anthropologists themselves sometimes do. But as I have put it before, that does not mean we have to admit complete defeat, as we would if we were all isolated in intellectual spaces between which no communication whatsoever is possible.

Yet that clearly obliges us to say what understanding across ontological regimes is possible, and how that can be achieved. We can make a start by observing that each regime implies radically different perceptions not just about whatever counts as reality, but also, as we said, on such key concepts as person, agency and causation. This does not mean that we can understand nothing of any set of assumptions on such issues that do not tally with our own antecedent convictions. Rather we should accept that those notions of ours are subject to revision and indeed set about doing just that, not necessarily abandoning our previous views but coming to appreciate other possibilities. In this way the fact that the ideas reported can be construed as relating to personhood and the like provides us with what I have called bridgeheads of intelligibility (Lloyd 2010b: 210). Of course our explorations cannot be undertaken with the impossible ambition of ourselves identifying with a shaman who crosses between worlds, or even with the members of societies where shamans have such an important role to fulfil – any more than we seek to identify with a Plato or a Socrates (however much some modern philosophers may wish to treat them as colleagues). But certainly we can entertain the aim, in each case, of broadening our knowledge of the range of human experience.

The particular point I would now emphasise is that the role of analogies in these ontological regimes is crucial. While Descola highlighted their pervasiveness in what he dubbed analogistic regimes, we should notice how his other three schemata still use and indeed make heavy use of continuities, which can be glossed as appreciating similarities, including analogies, between what is thought of as continuous. In that way they certainly do not dispense with analogy altogether. The continuity postulated in physicality (in naturalism) or in interiority (as in animism) or in both (as in totemism) evidently presupposes connections. True, two of the other three regimes (animism and naturalism) also incorporate, indeed make much of, discontinuities, differences, radical breaks, between humans and non-humans. But that just means that in those cases the reach of the urge to connect finds its distinctive limits, where animism is concerned in the discontinuities in physicalities, and where naturalism is concerned, in those of interiorities.

Equally, in Viveiros de Castro's perspectivism the likenesses and unlikenesses between humans and other beings are key. Jaguars and human beings both enjoy social relations with their conspecifics, but differ because of the bodies they have, and that in turn means that the experiences those bodies give them access to, their worlds indeed, are profoundly different. We have yet another example of the twin points I have made before. Which

likenesses are perceived as salient varies. But that likenesses of some particular kind will be thought salient does not.[24]

But if analogies, similarities, continuities are all-pervasive, that does
nothing to alleviate the problem of determining which ones are reliable,
which false friends. Two ways out of the impasse present drastic, but
hopelessly oversimplified, solutions. One opts for a radical scepticism, if
not solipsism, the other continues in the vain search for a unique solution.
A third option is to acknowledge that no such solution is possible but to
engage in the exploration of divergent but complementary models.

The sceptical turn starts from the valid observation that there is no
theory-free description to be given of whatever it is we wish to investigate.
But from that the sceptic will go on to conclude that there is no mind-
independent reality there to be accessed. That suggestion comes in different
forms and has generated a vast philosophical literature. Appeals in the Dr
Johnson mode, of kicking a table to show it is there, cut no ice. Our
foot and the table and the meeting of the two might still exist just in
our imagination. Nor will the sceptic be impressed by reference to what
science tells us about the molecular constitution of the table, or how our
feet have evolved, let alone about such matters as the age of different types
of geological structure. A determined objector will continue to protest that
the common-sense view begs the question.

Aristotle, faced with the view that had been expressed by one of his
predecessors, Parmenides, to the effect that change does not exist, pointed
out the difficulty of refuting that view. The problem he identified was that
any refutation, if it did not simply presuppose that change exists – and
so beg the question – had to proceed on some other basis. But that is
not possible since there is no other basis that is *clearer* than the facts of
perceptible change from which those facts could be shown. The sought-for
basis is always going to be more problematic than what it is supposed to be
grounds for. A similar reply will not satisfy someone determined to deny
any mind-independent reality: but then probably nothing would. There is
indeed a parting of the ways. The assertion that there is nothing there after
all, simply our imaginings, does not cut the Gordian knot so much as walk
away from the issue. The solipsist remains in splendid but barren isolation.
The rest of us will continue to identify problems to be investigated, many
of them intractable ones, but not take the easy way out of denying that
there is any work to be done.

---

[24] But if likenesses are crucial, so too are differences. Some would argue that that starts with the
boundaries between affines and cognates, on which the reproduction of human society depends
(cf. Vilaça 2013).

The second pitfall involves following the lead of naturalist imperialism that I have already criticised, in supposing that there is some unique definitive solution to be had to the issues about reality by which we are surrounded. The argument here is that we have no option but to proceed on the basis of our own conceptual assumptions which provide, accordingly, the limits of what we can comprehend. But to that the answer I have offered is that even our fundamental concepts are revisable, and that very revisability opens up the possibility of understanding even initially radically counter-intuitive ontological regimes. Revisability, on my view, so far from being a threat to mutual understanding, is its precondition.

Certainly recent and some not so recent anthropological explorations introduce us to what are for most of us totally new modes of existence, just as certain aspects of modern science can be said to have done, though in that case that is more often to do with the furniture of the world than with how we, as humans, can or should live within it. We learn from the anthropologists that we need to modify what we previously assumed about what counts as a person, as an agent, as a cause, even as space.[25] These divergent ontologies give us access to moral as well as cosmological views and ways of being in the world that are totally unfamiliar to us. But as we become a little more familiar with them, that enables us to expand and modify our own initial views, as we face the challenging task of learning from other people how they resolve problems about the human condition and about the reality that condition confronts.

Let me draw the threads of my argument together and end this chapter by recapitulating where reasonably confident answers or clarifications to the major issues seem possible and where they remain out of reach. Over a wide range of phenomena the natural sciences provide the most useful methods and the richest resources to answer the question of what there is. But science has its limits. First there are subject-areas where the (empirical) evidence available to us now is lacking. We cannot, as we said, access the first microsecond of the universe after the Big Bang, where both data and theory break down. Indeed we can only access parts of the distant – and

---

[25] Levinson (2003) identified three different systems of spatial coordinates that are attested, singly or in combination, in different human groups. In the first, the 'intrinsic' system, the coordinates are determined by the 'inherent features', sidedness or facets of the object to be used as the ground or relatum (e.g. the boy is in front of the house). The second, relative, frame of reference presupposes a viewpoint (given by the location of the perceiver) and a figure and ground distinct from that (e.g. the boy is to the left of the house, viz. from one viewpoint). Thirdly, there is the absolute frame of reference, found in many societies in different parts of the world, in which the coordinates are given by cardinal points such as north and south. I used this as an example of multidimensionality in Lloyd (2007a: ch. 2).

past – universe from which some information of some kind can reach us. The fossil record from which the evolution of the eukaryotes can be plotted is full of gaps. That genes are plastic is well known, but how that plasticity works out in practice is still not fully understood. In some cases the shortfall in the present evidence may be made up, but in others it may never be.

Secondly, and connectedly, there are instances where the obstacles are not merely contingent, but necessary or inevitable. The most famous example of that is Heisenberg's uncertainty principle which states that we cannot simultaneously determine both the momentum and the location of an elementary particle.

Then, thirdly, there are areas of our experience that currently fall outside the domain of the main established natural sciences altogether. Maybe psychiatry will one day be able to do more than just describe the degree of the severity of mental illnesses, but at present it merely offers generalisations, with no causal accounts to explain why treatments succeed, if and when they do. Neurophysiology sheds light on what happens in our brains and our nervous system when we experience emotions. But the emotions cannot be identified with, that is reduced to, what fMRI scans reveal. As Aristotle already pointed out, when we feel anger certain changes occur in our body (he spoke of the boiling of the blood about the heart: we might substitute a story of increased pulse rate, breathing, perspiration and so on). But those physical correlates are not what anger is, which is to be answered rather in terms of a reaction to a slight, to an injustice or what have you. Injustice is not just something we dream up, but it is not a given determinate species of behaviour.

'What there is' cannot be reduced to physical items, processes, interactions.[26] What in Descola's classification was put on the side of interiority, feelings, the self, has certainly to be included, though not necessarily in quite the way he suggested, which may savour too much of a residual Cartesian or Platonic mind–body dualism. That mode of contrasting the mental or the spiritual with the physical depended on a notion of an incorporeal substance and was open to the objection that the mind, once ontologically separated off from the body, has no way in which it can interact with it.[27] However we resolve the thorny question of mind–body relations, we must certainly acknowledge such interactions.

---

[26] That is not to deny that some reductions are possible, as when chemical interactions can be analysed in terms of molecular or atomic structures and interactions. However, evidently there are many aspects of our experience that are not to be explained in similar physical terms.

[27] As was famously argued by Ryle (1949).

The spheres of feelings and of morality are not amenable to the techniques of investigation favoured by the natural sciences. As we said, we can take certain measurements of neurophysiological events: but they are not what emotions are. Right and wrong are not quantifiable: we cannot conduct experiments to test hypotheses about morality, though developmental psychologists can indeed assess how children acquire some sense of equity.

What we mainly rely on, here, to achieve a better understanding, is, after all, analogy. Aristotle, in one of his rare moments of appreciation of metaphor that I mentioned before, wrote that skill in its use was a mark of genius and cannot be taught (*Poetics* 1459a5–8). That may well be a conclusion with which we ultimately have to agree. But a more optimistic opinion would be that we can get better at it if we apply ourselves to the task, to finding similarities where none had appeared initially, and to appreciating others that others propose, a practice that should also carry the advantage that we can come to understand one another better. This opens up a space for us to learn from what ethnography, and indeed ancient history, can tell us.

This does not mean that we agree with what others have believed on moral issues or on physical or cosmological ones. That is indeed impossible when those beliefs are mutually contradictory, although the occasions when we are dealing with well-formed formulae to which we can apply the Laws of Non-Contradiction and of Excluded Middle are far rarer than is often imagined in the discussions of philosophers. Certainly the key components of the cosmological views reported by Descola and Viveiros de Castro are well beyond the reach of a direct application of those laws, for they cannot be encapsulated in such well-formed formulae. But that in turn means that we have to exercise our imaginations if we are to learn and to apply what we learn.

Where questions of morality are involved, especially, we must understand before we criticise and reject. But comprehending does not mean condoning, even while the exercise of attempting to understand what we do not eventually condone is a salutary one and one from which, on the way, we can come to recognise aspects of our own moral assumptions of which we were not previously aware.

So the principal components of the provisional resolution of the ontological problems I have been exploring are those that I have introduced before. To escape both the solipsist trap and the imperialist pretensions of naturalism we need to recognise the multidimensionality of reality, the semantic stretch of the terms we have to use to capture it, and the radical revisability of any conceptual framework. Multidimensionality does not mean that reality is incoherent: semantic stretch does not imply that the range of application is limitless: revisability does not entail suspension of all judgement. Adopting those principles means hard work, in most cases harder work than we are generally used to, when we assume there are simple facts of the matter that will provide us with clear criteria for when our conclusions are true. But my submission is that we need some such principles if we are to do justice to the complexities of the problems of interpretation that we face in the study both of ancient thought and of the rich materials provided by ethnography. My final chapter will endeavour to survey the overall conclusions of my explorations and in the process to take stock of how we should assess our inheritance from Western philosophy and science.

Supplementary note: on Greek and Chinese ontologies and language

One of the most sustained attempts to identify general features of ancient Chinese and Greek thought and to relate them to aspects of the languages in which that thought was expressed comes in Graham (1989: Appendix 2, pp. 389–428). Inspired by Hansen's speculations (1983) that in classical Chinese nouns show greater affinity to the mass nouns of Indo-European languages than to count nouns, Graham argued that the tendency in classical Chinese thought is to start from the whole and to divide downwards, while in ancient Greek (and he considered most Western) thought the starting-point tends to be the particular from which wholes – the universe itself included – are constructed by aggregation.

Hansen had originally used his conjecture to help explicate one of the paradoxes of Gongsun Long (third century BCE) which states *bai ma fei ma*, usually translated 'a white horse is not a horse', but rendered by Hansen without the indefinite article, 'white horse is not horse' – so that the relationship that was denied was not class membership but the identity of two terms with distinct extensions. While Graham came to express his reservations about this analysis (Graham 1989: 83 and 401) he developed on his own account the view that Chinese 'divide down' while the Greeks 'add up'. The first problem with this thesis is that in both the Chinese and Greek cases it generalises over thinkers who themselves adopted very different views on this general issue. Plato would be one important counter-example on the Greek side, first in that for him the universal is certainly prior ontologically to the particular, and then in that his method of collection and division certainly uses both moves, for a prior collection, which at a pinch could be considered an 'adding up', is followed by a subsequent division, which definitely 'divides down'. On the Chinese side, conversely, an intense interest in class membership, and what items belong to the same class, is attested in cosmology (in the *Huainanzi*, for instance), in mathematics (see above, Chapter 4) and elsewhere.

In the background, of course, is the general issue of the relationship between thought and language, discussed from many different points of view by Vygotsky (1986), Carruthers (1996), Jackendoff (1996) and Chomsky (2006) among many others. The thesis that language guides and constrains thought, maybe even determines it, is associated especially with Sapir (1949) and Whorf (1967), and in the specific Chinese context with Bloom (1981) and Hall and Ames (1987) among others. The more extreme views ascribed to Sapir and Whorf, for example that the Hopi were incapable of making temporal distinctions, are easily refuted (cf. Wardy 2000), though whether either of them was fully committed to such positions has recently been called into question (Leavitt 2011). The point that should be retained is that certain semantic and syntactical features of a given natural language may help to make certain distinctions salient. Thus colour vocabulary may serve to call attention to certain differences even though there is extensive experimental evidence to show (if indeed it needs showing) that discriminations are possible without terms to describe them (Lloyd 2007a: ch. 1).

Meanwhile the fundamental point remains: any attempt to derive Greek or Chinese philosophical concepts from features of their natural languages faces the major difficulty of the very diversity in those concepts themselves, all expressed in either case in the same language.

CHAPTER 6

Conclusions

I began my Introduction by identifying some of the characteristic ambitions of the philosophy and science that have been developed largely in the West and by posing some of the problems that have increasingly been raised, in recent years, about aspects of those ambitions. Where do the ideals adopted by Western philosophy and science represent the key to greater understanding and to greater human welfare, thereby justifying the grandiose claims sometimes made for them? Where, on the contrary, are they open to criticism, distracting or downright misguided? How, in any event, are we to come to terms with the fact – when it is a fact – that these were historical developments associated particularly with the West and in many cases part of the heritage from ancient Greece? It is time now to take stock and to get the points both of the triumphalists and of their critics into perspective.

First a recapitulation of my main arguments is in order before I rehearse some of the objections that a more traditional view would mount. We asked, in Chapter 1, What are the conditions of possibility for translation and understanding? Obviously they cannot be perfect, but they are certainly not completely beyond our reach. Of course we have to start with our existing concepts, but I have insisted on their revisability. The difficulties we encounter are not insuperable barriers to communication, but rather incentives to learn. Assessment is inevitable, but that does not mean that we have a monopoly of the criteria by which everyone else is to be judged, for comparisons, as I argued in Chapter 2, should be even-handed. Often, as I showed with Greek and Chinese examples in Chapter 3, what are being compared are rival analogies, images and models, but it is a mistake to insist on replacing these everywhere with direct statements that conform to the standard requirements of univocity set down by Platonic and Aristotelian definition. Analogies may indeed mislead, but as Chapter 4 illustrated, they are a crucial resource for expanding our understanding. Faced with a plethora of rival accounts, ancient and modern, of ontologies or what there is, we should not assume that a single definitive solution should be our goal. Reality, I have argued throughout, is multidimensional and the terms we use to capture its different facets exhibit semantic stretch. I have brought to bear those two notions, of multidimensionality and semantic stretch, in suggesting that revisions are needed not just in our understanding of 'colour' and 'space', for example, but also of 'nature', 'animal', 'human', 'person', 'agency' and 'causation'.

Yet against all of that, many would claim that science and philosophy have only progressed in the ways they have because univocity and rigour have been demanded. We must have clear and precise definitions, many assume, otherwise we are lost. Ideally these should take the form of identifying the genus and giving the differentia. Again we must have strict demonstration, for mere persuasiveness or plausibility is not enough. Demonstrations should combine true premises (Aristotle thought the ultimately primary ones should include definitions and axioms) with valid deductive argument for which we need, of course, a clear concept of validity. Measurement, the replicability of experimentation, statistical analysis and computer modelling (to mention some of the styles that Hacking, e.g. 1992, 2009, 2012, has discussed) all have their fundamental contribution to make if we want our results to be robust.

Several of these styles and the ways they are now used are, of course, peculiarly modern. Some do not antedate the twentieth century, some go back only to the so-called 'scientific revolution' of the seventeenth century. But some of the key practices and notions that are still influential today go back, I have claimed, to the ancient Greeks. That is true particularly of the bid to give axiomatic-deductive demonstrations on the mathematical model and, where concepts are concerned, of the dichotomies between nature and culture, between realism and relativism (at least in one version) and between the literal and the metaphorical. The first of those pairs can be said to originate with Greek natural philosophers and doctors of the sixth and fifth centuries BCE: Plato provides a clear exposition of the second, and Aristotle was the first to drive a wedge between the literal and the metaphorical. So let me first broach the question of the particular circumstances in ancient Greece in which these developments occurred, while acknowledging that such an issue (like those to do with the 'scientific revolution' itself) is not going to yield to any simple resolution.

However, some hints of possibly relevant factors may be gleaned by comparing that other ancient civilisation that I have repeatedly invoked, namely China.[1] We have seen plenty of evidence of hard-hitting debate in ancient China, especially between those who competed for the ear of rulers and who tried to persuade them or their ministers to accept their advice. The exceptional feature of Greek debates is that they are often held before a lay audience and were indeed adjudicated by that audience. That applies to intellectual discussions (as on the constitution of the human body reported in the Hippocratic treatise *On the Nature of Man*), which themselves were partly modelled on the debates held in the political assemblies and law-courts, where the outcome was decided by a mass audience voting on the questions. It was in those circumstances that first Plato and then Aristotle demanded that arguments should be more than merely persuasive (for in their rather jaundiced opinion a lay audience could be persuaded of more or less anything, whether true or not, whether in the true interests of the state or not). So they insisted on proof, in Plato's case, and in Aristotle's on his notion of strict axiomatic-deductive demonstration that we have discussed. My argument would be not that the intellectual developments were determined by the political circumstances of ancient Greece, but at least that those circumstances provided an important stimulus, as we can see from the preoccupation of both Plato and Aristotle with the dangers of 'mere' persuasion. The Chinese, by contrast, did not demand incontrovertibility, but then they had no experience of the rival model that Plato and Aristotle shied away from, of decisions being taken by majority vote, where each vote counted the same as every other. As I pointed out, in mathematics, in particular, where we might have expected it, they made no attempt at axiomatisation. They checked their algorithms, for sure, but once they had reassured themselves that they were correct, they got on with the next problem.

The notes of caution concerning the value of those developments that my studies of ancient Greek thought suggest to me relate first to where there is a temptation to ignore or downplay the possible drawbacks of some of those demands for rigour. When is it appropriate to try to base an inquiry on self-evident, indemonstrable primary premises? When is definition *per genus et differentiam* indeed what we should aim for? Can we always be confident that reliable genera and differentiae are indeed to be found in the subject-matter we are investigating? In one of the subject-areas that has stood as a paradigm example of the importance, even the necessity, of such definitions, that is the classification of animals, modern taxonomy

[1] For a fuller discussion of the arguments that follow in this paragraph I may refer to Lloyd (2014: ch. 1).

has, as we have seen, to admit the limits of the applicability of those earlier ambitions, at least where large swathes of the animal kingdom are concerned. Cladistics provides us with a subtler mode of classification than the dichotomous division Aristotle criticised, but every mode of ordering the eukaryotes runs into difficulties sooner or later. Is that just a matter that at present we do not know enough, that there are gaps in our evidence? Maybe. But for now the belief that a clear definitive picture will eventually emerge is an expression of faith, and what that picture will look like is quite unpredictable.

True, there are many other areas of science where results are unlikely to be overturned, as for example concerning the large-scale structure of the universe, the analysis of the human gene, and perhaps especially basic chemistry. But even in that last case the conventional formula for water as H_2O that we all accept was for long far from a foregone conclusion. The story has been told in meticulous detail by Hasok Chang (2012) who pointed out how open, initially, was the debate between the proponents of H_2O and those who favoured a different view of the hydrogen component, which gave the formula HO. The victory of the former depended on a number of decisions where they successfully imposed their views over those of their rivals. Chang even maintains that there are points still worth exploring in the defeated option.

Moreover being H_2O is not all we need to know about water. Let me go back to the Chinese and Greek data to illustrate this and to point out how diagnoses of mistakes should wait on full explorations of the senses and referents of the relevant terms. One complication of assessing Chinese *shui* arises from the comment in the text I cited that it 'means' or 'says' 'soaking downwards'. In other words it here names a process rather than a substance. A text in the *Lüshi chunqiu* (1/2/2) adds a further consideration, for it says that the *xing* (the characteristic) of water (*shui* again) is 'purity' (*qing*). That is baffling until we read on, for the text continues that the *xing* of humans (*ren*) is 'long life' (*shou²*). Clearly this author is concerned with ideals, not with necessary and sufficient conditions. But we would only judge him wrong if we mistakenly thought he was interested in saying what the substance of water is.

On the Greek side *hudōr* ('water') was evidently primordial for Thales, who according to Aristotle (*Metaphysics* 983b20–7) associated it with life. When Pindar said that 'water is best' (*Olympians* 1 1), better even than gold, he too may have had in mind its importance for life. Aristotle's treating water as a 'simple body' looks more familiar (and mistaken) but even here there are complications. He knows that it exists not just as a liquid but as a solid, ice, and as steam, but he also claims (*Meteorologica* 358b16–359a3) that sea water and wine when evaporated turn into 'water'. In the first case he describes putting a closed jar in the sea (the text talks of a wax jar, *kērinon*, but a plausible emendation is an earthenware, *keraminon*, one) whereupon after a time drops of water will be found in it. In the case of wine he says that there too when the liquid is evaporated and subsequently condensed it becomes water. One interpretation is that he never carried out the tests, although he expressly says he did. But if the evaporate of the heated wine was collected on a metal lid, the resultant would be a colourless, tasteless, liquid of low alcoholic content, that he would treat as 'water' just as much as the evaporate from sea water (such as might be collected in an earthenware jar) would be 'drinkable', *potimon*, *hudōr*. Simply diagnosing error in such cases would be mistakenly to import modern anachronistic notions of chemically pure substances into our interpretations. Chemical analysis is good for what it is: but, to repeat, it does not tell us all we need to know about the substances in question.

When we turn from science to philosophy, to ethics for instance, Socrates' demand that he should be given not instances of courage, but what courage is essentially, assumes that there is just the one definitive answer to that question. During the course of his discussion with his inter-locutors, they learn that courage in battle is only one type, courage in the face of sickness is another, and so on. But should we suppose that we shall ever get to the end of the process of learning what courage is? When can we be satisfied that the job has been completed? Human experience in general, as well as our own personal experience, can and does expand and grow. If and when we think we have come to an end of the trail, how are we to encapsulate what we have learned on the way?

Aristotle thought that the courage shown by animals is not true courage (since that, for him, depended on moral choice). We can understand the argument and yet dissent from his conclusion, as indeed would many of his fellow Greeks for whom lions of course were paradigms of courage.[2] Again it is not at all straightforward to say where courage shades off into rashness, nor when it depends on a complete knowledge of the relevant facts of the situation. When does an instantaneous reaction, an unthinking one as we

---

[2] Indeed Aristotle himself treats lions as paradigms of courage in his discussion of physiognomical inference, *Prior Analytics* II ch. 27, where he considers whether there might be a particular physical characteristic that could be used as an indicator of character. In the zoological works, too, when he discusses animals' characters, he gives lions as examples of 'courageous' creatures without qualification (*History of Animals* 488b17). The extent to which that traditional Greek view reflected first-hand knowledge of lions is a moot point. Less powerful creatures, including ordinary cats, defending their young against attack, might be better examples of courage in animals.

say, not count as courage? Compare Mencius' example (as discussed above in Chapter 3). He spoke of our instinctive reaction to save a child from falling down a well, but he used that as a reason for asserting that humans are inherently good. But exposure to philosophical argument (let alone to actual lions, or to children about to fall down wells – in practice or just in a thought experiment) surely expands our view and modifies what we understand by courage. Definitions should be thought of as starting-points for further explorations and may need to be revised as we learn more: to seek to give definitive accounts, as Socrates often seemed to demand, is liable to suggest prematurely that the matter can then be closed.

I have identified some of the problems that stem from a demand or an expectation of univocity, from an insistence on literality, and have proposed that semantic stretch is a pervasive feature of language. That does not mean that we remain in a state of permanent suspended judgement. We may think the Socratic programme to be a mirage, but that certainly does not stop us learning from Plato's dramatic presentations of him. We can ponder the implications of Aristotle on courage and Mencius on the good and enrich our understanding of courage and goodness, without setting as our goal some understanding that will be final, let alone one that can be neatly summed up in a single formula.

Science is subject to greater checks and controls than moral philosophy, but in science too we must certainly be wary of assuming that no further revision of our conclusions or of our basic conceptual framework will ever be called for. This acceptance of revisability is so much less comfortable than our habit of demanding, from parents or teachers or colleagues, that they give us plain answers to all our not so plain questions. Demands for clarification should be met within the limits of which we are capable and – just as importantly – as far as the subject permits, though there is no way in which we can predict where that limit comes. Protesting that the subject is difficult can be just evasive: but pressing for simplicity or for certainty can be deeply mistaken. Ambiguity is undeniably an impediment to communication. But univocity can be a misplaced ideal. To go down the Aristotelian route of insisting, in many and the most important contexts, on the literal, and banning what he called the metaphorical, is to deny ourselves a major resource for increasing our understanding.

As we have seen over and over again, and is just obvious, we constantly use comparisons and contrasts to make sense of our experience. We are for ever spotting or suggesting or inventing similarities, and just as often, and sometimes *ipso facto*, identifying differences and insisting on contrasts. We are all aware (usually at least) that the similarities we think we perceive or recognise may be deceptive and on many more occasions may be plain uninformative or trivial.[3] Moreover, in our communications with others, our partners in dialogue, we sometimes sense that they may be manipulating those similarities and even may do so intentionally to deceive us. There was, as we have documented, no need of Western philosophy or science or literature to arrive at such a realisation, since it is abundantly attested across the populations of the world. In this instance the experience of China parallels that of Greece rather than contrasts with it. Conversely we can become aware of the likenesses between things that we initially mistakenly categorised as antithetical. But those awarenesses are all very well. The constant problem is to sift the genuine, the useful, the objective, similarities and differences from the misleading ones.

How is that to be done? Of course there is no sure-fire rule for that. But some observations about what we can reasonably expect may not be misplaced. The urge for definitive solutions should be tempered with a due realisation of the possibility of pluralism. In the instances of multidimensionality I have discussed it is a mistake (so I argue) to opt for a single account to the exclusion of others. They may deal with different facets of a complex subject-matter, though to see whether or how they do requires, precisely, careful analysis of similarities and differences. The case of colour that is one of the main examples I have used shows this (I hope) comparatively uncontroversially.

Where complex ontological regimes are concerned, the problems are appreciably more difficult, since what each regime is committed to and what it rules out is often opaque. However, it is possible, following Descola's lead, to make some progress in grasping different perspectives on interiorities and physicalities. But that would not be with the aim of settling the issues in favour of *one* solution to how those should be construed, but rather to explore what we can learn from each. Where attempts are made explicitly to raise, and to justify with philosophical arguments the answers to, questions to do with reality as a whole, the need to entertain the possibility of multidimensionality is particularly great, not least because of the exclusive ambitions of unique solutions. The alternative to those is not mere relativism, for I have suggested that the simple view that represents the choice between that and realism as one between mutually exclusive and exhaustive alternatives can be countered.

---

[3] After all a similarity of a purely trivial kind may be asserted between *any* two items whatsoever simply by saying that they have been mentioned together. Only slightly more substantially Hamlet has no difficulty in getting Polonius to agree that 'yonder cloud' is like a camel, like a weasel and like a whale ('very like a whale') (*Hamlet* Act 3, scene 2).

One of the cornerstones of Western modernity, we said, has been the assumption of the dichotomy between nature and culture. Here my tactics have been to expose the asymmetry between the pair. 'Nature', my argument is, is not a given, and that in two senses. First it is not in fact found universally as an explicit concept that is recognised in every language, and again I used ancient China to make the point, though that was not to deny that the Chinese, like everyone else, recognised some regularities in some phenomena, including some we would class as 'natural' phenomena – though as I noted before, manifesting some regularity does not imply belonging to the domain we call 'nature'. Secondly, what is there to be investigated is not a single given reality, but open-ended and, as I have put it, multidimensional.

The acceptance of the universality of 'culture', conversely, registers, on the one hand, that humans are indeed social beings, and on the other allows space for diverging views about norms and practices and beliefs, about what it is to be a human being as well as about what it is that as humans we face, the world we inhabit. Ideas on such fundamental issues are not only not immune to error (often in the form of oversimplification), but may be particularly prone to it. We cannot settle for the view that each is correct on its own terms and that there is no possibility of evaluating them. True, we can never stand outside all of our own assumptions. But we should be prepared to challenge any one of them. It is only if we believe that each system is mutually unintelligible to others that no evaluation is possible and we have seen reason to reject that assumption. Different societies or groups or simply individuals have entertained what on the face of it appear highly counter-intuitive solutions or strategies for understanding and for living. But that just means we have to work harder to understand. We are used, maybe, to trying to make sense of the strange ideas of Parmenides or Plato or Kant or Zhuangzi or Mozi.[4] The cosmological regimes reported by the anthropologists introduce us to an even greater range of beliefs and practices that whole communities entertain. But Cannibal Metaphysics, as Viveiros de Castro puts it (2009), poses analogous hermeneutic challenges as other metaphysics.

So we come back to those features of Western modernity with which we began. The methodological tools that it has deployed – and which I

---

[4] Mozi is one of many Chinese thinkers I have not dealt with at all adequately in my discussion here. The texts associated with his name, dating from the fourth to the start of the first century BCE, go further into the question of the basis of knowledge than any other extant classical Chinese writings, but they ceased to have much influence on subsequent Chinese thought until they were rediscovered in the nineteenth century.

have spent a good deal of my discussion criticising – have undeniably been responsible for remarkable increases in knowledge and control, indeed far beyond what any ancient Greek could have imagined, when we think of those robust achievements of modern science. Although I have pointed out that the demands for rigour, for univocity, for demonstration, can be misplaced, they have often been instrumental in sharpening critical evaluation of assumptions about the physical environment, about morality, about religion, although they have also led to too hasty a dismissal of other ways of knowing.

The possibility of radical criticism depended and depends on favourable political and ideological conditions, as well as intellectual ones, of course. We tend to believe that egalitarian societies are more open and more self-critical than autocratic ones, for the principle that everyone has an equal say can be extended from the political to other domains. We like to think of democratic Athens as a particularly favourable environment for free speech, and so indeed it may have been, though we should not forget that it executed Socrates, that it imposed imperial rule over its erstwhile allies and often put down their rebellions with great savagery, and that it was because they opposed democratic institutions, not because they applauded them, that Plato and Aristotle forged the new ideals for inquiry that they did, with the complex consequences that I have charted. Democratic audiences can be as stubborn, as narrow-minded and as bigoted as any autocratic monarch.

As for modern democracies, the main flaw they suffer from (as I argued in Lloyd 2004) is that politicians, conscious that they will soon come up for re-election, often take lamentably short-term views. They assume that their constituents are chiefly, maybe even exclusively, concerned with their own material welfare and may not even extend that concern to others, let alone adopt any loftier or more spiritual ideals. I would not argue that any other political regime is superior to 'democracy'. But the problem is to make some version of it work and that would seem to depend first of all on a massive transformation in the quality of political debate as well as on a more serious engagement, by the citizen-body as a whole, in the political process.

There is of course absolutely no guarantee that in politics or anywhere else measured judgements will come increasingly to prevail. Changes in political thinking follow changes in the relationships of power and the ability to coerce more often than they do philosophical or even just commonsensical reflections (Cf. Runciman 2009). The history of science itself, and not just in the West, is full of examples where new ideas that seem to us to have the balance of argument in their favour were not accepted by contemporaries. Our local environment does not immediately endorse the idea that the earth is spherical. Again the rejection of heliocentricity when it was first proposed by Aristarchus was not just foolish, for from the point of view of an observer on earth, the sun does indeed circle the earth: we do not see the earth rotating when we see the sun set. The history of what eventually came to seem obvious has been punctuated by doubts and disputes, from the sphericity of the earth and heliocentricity, through Darwinian evolution, right down to DNA and plate tectonics, and the doubters were not always diehard traditionalists fighting some rearguard, ideologically loaded action.

Again the pursuit of the correct understanding of the causes of diseases has led not just to new knowledge but to previously unimagined possibilities for treatment. The Malaria goddess is irrelevant to malaria: the Anopheles mosquito is not. You cannot do much to placate the goddess, though you may believe your rituals will help and, if performed with due felicity, may offer you some psychological comfort. But you can eradicate mosquitoes.

In such instances, where Western biomedicine confronts alternative systems, it may seem to many that the correctness of the one and the errors of the others are a foregone conclusion. Yet even in such cases it is as well for Western biomedicine to acknowledge its own limitations, not just in its understanding of particular diseases, but in its ability to produce a cure, but then even further than that, in its comprehension of what its patients need for their full well-being, in its understanding of what health itself comprises – a semantically stretched term if ever there was one. If some would settle for the absence of any pathological condition or obvious disability – you are healthy if you are not physically ill or disabled – others (including myself) would insist that there is more to being healthy than that, that health is a matter of well-being, of flourishing, where we should take into account not just the conditions of our bodies (our physicalities) but also our minds (our interiorities). Some would even argue that true well-being is not possible in an unjust society. This is not to say that traditional herbal remedies are as good as or even better than their chemically synthesised counterparts (though that may sometimes be the case: cf. Hsu 2010). But it does remind us of the complexities that we all sense in the ways in which lives can be well led.

Without Western science and philosophy, where would we be? Certainly without the gadgets, the pills and the ironically named creature comforts that most of us take for granted. With less scientific knowledge to be sure, but with a better understanding of ourselves and of how to live together?

Not necessarily, but not necessarily a worse. With the advances that have been made in both the natural and the social sciences, one might suppose that that would have led not just to greater material prosperity but also to general welfare. But evidently the record, in the latter regard particularly, has been patchy. There are few signs of any end to human misery, and none of any immediate end to fanaticism.

One problem is easily identifiable. Insofar as welfare depends on how human social, national and increasingly nowadays international relations are organised, that demands not just knowledge but action. The greater the impact we have on our environment, the more urgent those questions become, where understanding is undeniably crucial, but determination to act on that understanding is even more important. Promoting greater equity, justice, tolerance seems ever more difficult to achieve, not least because so many still deny that those are the aims we need to set ourselves. We may seek to insist on the positive values of fellow-feeling, of mutual understanding and support, but we have to be realistic about how deaf many people are to any such appeals and how the circumstances of rampant competitive materialism may militate against their realisation. Western philosophers, in the wake of Aristotle, demanded methods that would guarantee the certainty of their results. Monotheistic religions, not just Christianity, have kept the mirage of that ideal but generally secure it, not by argument,[5] but by appeal to some sacred text or set of dogmas, often with catastrophic effects for pluralism and tolerance.

That was one of the cases I took to illustrate where understanding others' views does not lead to accepting them. Yet we have first to understand them as well as we can, even and especially in the face of assertions that no outsider can even begin to comprehend the true nature of the divine. We should endeavour, nevertheless, to be aware of the tools our opponents use as well as the ones we do, for every religion, from dogmatic, highly institutionalised ones to personal expressions of spiritual experience, draws heavily on analogies, comparisons and symbolic associations. They provide some access to meaning, even when the faithful insist that the infidel can have no true understanding and faces damnation for that very reason. Moreover one thing that anyone can recognise, when they see it, is the intolerance that goes with that insistence.

One of my main themes has been that analogies have been and continue to be one of the principal cognitive resources humans everywhere

---

[5] However, as I noted before, Christian theologians certainly attempted demonstrations, including of the existence of God, often constructed on Aristotelian models, when they imagined that such demonstrations could be given.

deploy, indeed in every type of context. I have illustrated something of their immense variety, from Chinese resonances to Kepler, from Greek visions of the obscure to Aristotle's investigations of the animal kingdom (with Aristotle now figuring as explorer rather than as censor-in-chief) and including (I have suggested) the continuities, and so similarities, to be found in the ontological regimes reported in ethnography. Sometimes the relationships in question are covert and implicit, sometimes very much explicit, novel and suggestive, often highly charged emotionally, especially when the target for understanding is the divine, as we saw in Chapter 2. They can evidently be used or abused, supporting positive or negative goals even while they help us to see that the goals have different valences. For all these reasons, it is as well, then, to try to comprehend their power and their fallibility, but that does not, cannot, mean trying to immunise them against deceptiveness.

It is clear, for example, from several of the papers collected in Helman (1988), that many still hanker after a way to make analogical reasoning sound, so that the dangers of the pitfalls of negative analogies and of fallacious analogical argument just disappear. Yet that goal constantly eludes realisation, even when (and maybe even especially when) attempts at formalisation are made, including those that bring to bear artificial intelligence or computer modelling. I recognise that my own rejection of the literal in favour of semantic stretch may be thought to compound the problems, rendering them indeed insoluble, since insofar as terms are liable to stretch, we cannot set down definitive limits to their applicability.

But paradoxically, perhaps, the realisation of the insolubility of the problem as traditionally posed releases us from an impossible ambition, so that we can concentrate on the benefits that can be gained from investigations freed from that mirage. Analogies are always going to be potentially misleading. There is no cure for that. But that should not inhibit us from exploring them to the full, both our own and those we encounter in other groups or societies ancient or modern. If their potentiality to mislead is shocking, their potentiality to suggest connections is the best tool we have to increase both our own understanding – by revising and expanding our conceptual schemata – and our understanding of others and their ways of being in the world.

Plato was surely right when he described likenesses as a 'most slippery tribe'. But one group of them offers our best chance of cultivating the tolerance we so badly need, namely those that counter divisiveness and insist on what we and every other human being have in common. Even that encounters resistance, of course, from those who insist on their or their group's uniqueness. Against that, our best hope for pushing back the incursions of prejudice remains a resolute focus on commonalities, our shared biology, our shared use of language, our shared sociability, our shared sense of beauty and of wonder and awareness of death, even though what these 'sharings' consist in and how they manifest themselves are, as we have seen, in every case problematic. Terence famously proclaimed: 'humani nil a me alienum puto'.[6] The 'nil' here goes too far, since the evil that humans are capable of, in relation to other humans, is something that we must distance ourselves from. But learning what other humans cherish is the best aid to self-criticism that we can command.

[6] 'I deem nothing that is human to be foreign to me', Terence, *The Self-Tormentor* 76.

Glossary of Chinese terms

ba	肢	naked
bai ma fei ma	白馬非馬	(a) white horse is not (a) horse
bei	誖	inconsistent
ben	本	root
bi	比	compare, analogical poetry
bie lei	別類	different kinds
cao	草	grasses
chang	常	constant
chong	蟲	'insects'
chu	畜	domesticated animals
churu xiangbu	出入相補	'out–in complementary principle'
dan	彈	bow-like instrument
dao	道	The Way
dao ke dao fei chang dao	道可道非常道	The way that can spoken of is not the constant way
dongwu	動物	animal ('moving thing')
duan	端	starting-point, principle
gangji	綱紀	guiding principles
gou gu	句股	horizontal and vertical lines of a right-angled triangle
gu	故	reason, cause, therefore
junzi	君子	'gentleman'
lanming	覽冥	examining obscurities
lei	類	category
luo¹	裸	hairless
luo²	臝	hairless
mu	木	tree
niao	鳥	bird
qi¹	氣	breath, energy
qi²	齊	homogenise

qin	禽	bird
qing	清	pure, purity
qiwulun	齊物論	'The sorting which evens things out'
ren	人	human
Shang Di	上帝	The Lord on High
shao	韶	type of music
sheng[1]	生	life, produce
sheng[2]	勝	conquer
shou[1]	獸	animal, beast
shou[2]	壽	long life
shui	水	water
shuo	說	explain, persuade
tong	同	equalise
wu	舞	type of music
wu xing	五行	five phases
xian	弦	hypotenuse
xing	性	character
yang	羊	sheep/goats
yi[1]	義	morality
yi[2]	頤	(name of hexagram)
yi si	疑似	spurious resemblances
yin yang	陰陽	negative and positive principles
yu	魚	fish
yu yan	寓言	'lodge sayings'
yue	曰	say, mean
yue ling	月令	monthly ordinances
zhong	種	seed, kind

Notes on editions

Chinese texts are generally cited according to the standard editions, for example from the Harvard-Yenching Institute series (*Mengzi, Mozi, Xunzi, Zhuangzi*), the University of Hong Kong Institute of Chinese Studies series (*Daodejing, Erya, Gongsun Longzi, Hanfeizi, Liezi, Lunyu, Shanhaijing, Shangshu, Shuo Yuan, Yijing, Zhouli*) and the *Zhonghua shuju* dynastic histories. However, for *Huainanzi* I use the edition by Liu Wendian (Shanghai, 1923). For *Lüshi chunqiu* I use the edition by Chen Qiyou (Shanghai, 1984), but I adopt the chapter subdivisions in Knoblock and Riegel (Stanford, 2000) and for *Xunzi* I adopt the chapter subdivisions in Knoblock (Stanford 1988–94). For *Jiuzhang suanshu* and Liu Hui's commentary, and for *Zhoubi suanjing*, I use the edition of Qian Baocong, *Suanjing shishu* (Beijing, 1963).

Greek and Latin authors are similarly cited according to the standard editions, for example the Presocratic philosophers according to the edition of H. Diels, revised by W. Kranz, *Die Fragmente der Vorsokratiker*, 6th edn (Berlin, 1952), the works of Plato according to Burnet's Oxford text, and the treatises of Aristotle according to Bekker's Berlin edition. Greek medical texts are cited, for preference, in the *Corpus Medicorum Graecorum* (*CMG*) editions, and mathematical ones in the Teubner ones.

All modern works are cited by author's name and year of publication. Full details are to be found in the Bibliography that follows.

Bibliography

Adler, J. E. and Rips. L. J. (eds.) (2008) *Reasoning: Studies of Human Inference and its Foundations* (Cambridge).

Agassi, J. (1988) 'Analogies hard and soft', in Helman (1988), 401–19.

Aiton, E. J., Duncan, A. M. and Field, J. V. (1997) *The Harmony of the World by Johannes Kepler* (American Philosophical Society, vol. 209) (Philadelphia).

Allwood, J. and Gärdenfors, P. (1999) *Cognitive Semantics: Meaning and Cognition* (Amsterdam).

Arnauld, A. and Nicole, P. (1996 [1683]) *Logic or the Art of Thinking*, ed. and trans. J. V. Buroker from *La logique ou l'art de penser* (Cambridge).

Atran, S. (1990) *Cognitive Foundations of Natural History* (Cambridge).

(1995) 'Causal constraints on categories and categorical constraints on biological reasoning across cultures', in Sperber, Premack and Premack (1995), 205–33.

(1998) 'Folk biology and the anthropology of science: cognitive universals and cultural particulars', *Behavioral and Brain Sciences* 21: 547–609.

Atran, S., Medin, D. and Ross, N. (2004) 'Evolution and devolution of knowledge: a tale of two biologies', *Journal of the Royal Anthropological Institute NS* 10: 395–420.

Austin, J. L. (1962) *How To Do Things With Words* (Oxford).

Avital, E. and Jablonka, E. (2000) *Animal Traditions: Behavioural Inheritance in Evolution* (Cambridge).

Barkow, J. H., Cosmides, L. and Tooby, J. (eds.) (1992) *The Adapted Mind: Evolutionary Psychology and the Generation of Culture* (Oxford).

Barnes, S. B. (1973) 'The comparison of belief-systems: anomaly versus falsehood', in Horton and Finnegan (1973), 182–98.

Bergson, H. (1911 [1907]) *Creative Evolution*, trans. A. Mitchell from *L'évolution créatrice* (New York).

Berlin, B., Breedlove, D. E. and Raven, P. H. (1973) 'General principles of classification and nomenclature in folk biology', *American Anthropologist* 75: 214–42.

Berlin, B. and Kay, P. (1969) *Basic Color Terms: Their Universality and Evolution* (Berkeley).

Black, M. (1962) *Models and Metaphors* (Ithaca, N.Y.).

Bloom, A. H. (1981) *The Linguistic Shaping of Thought* (Hillsdale, N.J.).

Bourdieu, P. (2004 [2001]) *Science of Science and Reflexivity*, trans. R. Nice from *Science de la science et réflexivité* (Cambridge).

Boyd, R. and Richerson, P. J. (2005) *The Origin and Evolution of Cultures* (Oxford).

Boyer, P. (1995) 'Causal understanding in cultural representations: cognitive constraints on inferences from cultural input', in Sperber, Premack and Premack (1995), 615–44.

Brashier, K. E. (2011) *Ancestral Memory in Early China* (Cambridge, Mass.)

Bryan, J. (2012) *Likeness and Likelihood in the Presocratics and Plato* (Cambridge).

Buchdahl, G. (1972) 'Methodological aspects of Kepler's theory of refraction', *Studies in History and Philosophy of Science* 3: 265–98.

Burnyeat, M. F. (1982) 'The origins of non-deductive inference', in J. Barnes, J. Brunschwig, M. Burnyeat and M. Schofield (eds.) *Science and Speculation* (Cambridge), 193–238.

(1994) 'Enthymeme: Aristotle on the logic of persuasion', in D. J. Furley and A. Nehamas (eds.) *Aristotle's Rhetoric: Philosophical Essays* (Princeton, N.J.), 3–55.

(2000) 'Plato on why mathematics is good for the soul', in T. Smiley (ed.) *Mathematics and Necessity* (Oxford), 1–81.

Burstein, M. H. (1988) 'Combining analogies in mental models', in Helman (1988), 179–203.

Byrne, R. W. and Whiten, A. (eds.) (1988) *Machiavellian Intelligence* (Oxford).

Carey, S. (1985) *Conceptual Change in Childhood* (Cambridge, Mass.).

(2009) *The Origin of Concepts* (Oxford).

Carey, S. and Spelke, E. S. (1994) 'Domain-specific knowledge and conceptual change', in L. A. Hirschfeld and S. A. Gelman (eds.) *Mapping the Mind: Domain Specificity in Cognition and Culture* (Cambridge), 169–200.

Carrithers, M., Collins, S. and Lukes, S. (eds.) (1985) *The Category of the Person* (Cambridge).

Carruthers, P. (1996) *Language, Thought and Consciousness* (Cambridge).

Chang, H. (2012) *Is Water H_2O? Evidence, Realism and Pluralism* (Dordrecht).

Chemla, K. (ed.) (2012) *The History of Mathematical Proof in Ancient Traditions* (Cambridge).

Chemla, K. and Guo Shuchun (2004) *Les neuf chapitres: le classique mathématique de la Chine ancienne et ses commentaires* (Paris).

Cheng, F. (1979) 'Bi et xing', *Cahiers de Linguistique Asie Orientale* 6: 63–74.

Chomsky, N. (2006 [1968]) *Language and Mind*, 3rd edn (Cambridge).

Conklin, H. C. (1955) 'Hanunoo color terms', *Southwestern Journal of Anthropology* 11: 339–44.

Cooper, W. (2001) *The Evolution of Reason* (Cambridge).

Cosmides, L. and Tooby, J. (1992) 'Cognitive adaptations for social exchange', in Barkow, Cosmides and Tooby (1992), 163–228.

Crane, T. (1995) *The Mechanical Mind* (London).

Daston, L. and Galison, P. (2007) *Objectivity* (New York).

Daston, L. and Mitman, G. (eds.) (2005) *Thinking with Animals* (New York).

Davidson, D. (2001) *Essays on Actions and Events*, 2nd edn (Oxford).

De Jong, W. R. and Betti, A. (2010) 'The classical model of science: a millennia-old model of scientific rationality', *Synthèse* 174: 185–203.

Delpla, I. (2001) *Quine, Davidson: le principe de charité* (Paris).

Dennett, D. (1979) *Brainstorms* (Hassocks).

Denyer, N. (2007) 'Sun and line: the role of the good', in G. R. F. Ferrari (ed.) *The Cambridge Companion to Plato's Republic* (Cambridge), ch. 11, 284–309.

Descola, P. (2013 [2005]) *Beyond Nature and Culture*, trans. J. Lloyd from *Par-delà nature et culture* (Chicago).

Dijksterhuis, E. J. (1986) *The Mechanization of the World-Picture: Pythagoras to Newton* (Princeton, N.J.).

Diller, H. (1932) 'opsis adēlōn ta phainomena', *Hermes* 67: 14–42.

Donahue, W. H. (2000) *Johannes Kepler, Optics* (Santa Fe).

Dumont, L. (1986) *Essay on Individualism: Modern Ideology in Anthropological Perspective* (Chicago).

Dunbar, R. (1995) *The Trouble with Science* (London).

(1996) 'The social brain hypothesis', *Evolutionary Anthropology* 6: 178–90.

Dunbar, R., Knight, C. and Power, C. (eds.) (1999) *The Evolution of Culture* (Edinburgh).

Dupré, J. (1993) *The Disorder of Things* (Cambridge, Mass.).

(2001) 'In defence of classification', *Studies in History and Philosophy of Biological and Biomedical Sciences* 32: 203–19.

(2002) *Humans and Other Animals* (Oxford).

Durkheim, E. and Mauss, M. (1963 [1903]) *Primitive Classification*, trans. R. Needham from 'De quelques formes primitives de classification', *L'Année sociologique*, 1901–2 (London).

Evans, J. St.-B. T. (1989) *Bias in Human Reasoning* (Hove).

Evans-Pritchard, E. E. (1937) *Witchcraft, Oracles and Magic among the Azande* (Oxford).

(1956) *Nuer Religion* (Oxford).

Everett, D. L. (2012) *Language: The Cultural Tool* (London).

Feyerabend, P. K. (1975) *Against Method* (London).

Fisher, J. (1975) *The Magic of Lewis Carroll* (Harmondsworth).

Fodor, J. A. (1981) *Representations: Philosophical Essays on the Foundations of Cognitive Science* (Brighton).

Forster, M. N. (1998) 'On the very idea of denying the existence of radically different conceptual schemes', *Inquiry* 41: 133–85.

Fracasso, R. (1993) '*Shan hai ching*', in M. Loewe (ed.) *Early Chinese Texts: A Bibliographical Guide* (Early China Special Monograph Series 2) (Berkeley), 357–67.

Frazer, J. G. (1911–15) *The Golden Bough*, 12 vols., 3rd edn (London).

Gardner, M. (1956) *Mathematics, Magic and Mystery* (New York).

Geller, M. (2010) *Ancient Babylonian Medicine* (Chichester).

Gellner, E. (1973) 'The savage and the modern mind', in Horton and Finnegan (1973), 162–81.

(1988) *Plough, Sword and Book* (London).

(1998) *Language and Solitude: Wittgenstein, Malinowski and the Habsburg Dilemma* (Cambridge).

Gelman, S. A. and Byrnes, J. P. (eds.) (1991) *Perspectives on Language and Thought: Interrelations in Development* (Cambridge).

Gentner, D., Holyoak, K. J. and Kokinov, B. N. (eds.) (2001) *The Analogical Mind: Perspectives from Cognitive Science* (Cambridge, Mass.).

Gernet, J. (1985 [1982]) *China and the Christian Impact*, trans. J. Lloyd from *Chine et Christianisme* (Cambridge).

Ghiselin, M. T. (1966) 'On psychologism in the logic of taxonomic controversies', *Systematic Zoology* 15: 207–15.

(1974) 'A radical solution to the species problem', *Systematic Zoology* 23: 536–44.

(1997) *Metaphysics and the Origin of Species* (Albany, N.Y.).

Gigerenzer, G. and Goldstein, D. G. (1996) 'Reasoning the fast and frugal way: models of bounded rationality', *Psychological Review* 103: 650–69.

Gigerenzer, G. and Todd, P. M. (1999) *Simple Heuristics That Make Us Smart* (Oxford).

Gladstone, W. E. (1877) 'The colour sense', *The Nineteenth Century* 2: 360–88.

Goldin, P. R. (2008) 'The myth that China has no creation myth', *Monumenta Serica* 56: 1–22.

Goodman, N. (1978) *Ways of Worldmaking* (Hassocks).

Goody, J. (1977) *The Domestication of the Savage Mind* (Cambridge).

Graham, A. C. (1960) *The Book of Lieh-tzu* (London).

(1978) *Later Mohist Logic, Ethics and Science* (London).

(1989) *Disputers of the Tao* (La Salle, Ill.).

Griffin, D. R. (1984) *Animal Thinking* (Cambridge, Mass.).

(1992) *Animal Minds* (Chicago).

Hacking, I. (1992) '"Style" for historians and philosophers', *Studies in History and Philosophy of Science* 23: 1–20.

(2002) *Historical Ontology* (Cambridge, Mass.).

(2007) 'Natural kinds: rosy dawn, scholastic twilight', in A. O'Hear (ed.) *Philosophy of Science* (Cambridge), 203–39.

(2009) *Scientific Reason* (Taipei).

(2012) '"Language, truth and reason" 30 years later', *Studies in History and Philosophy of Science* 43: 599–609.

(2014) *Why Is There Philosophy Of Mathematics At All?* (Cambridge).

Hadot, P. (2006 [2004]) *The Veil of Isis: An Essay on the History of the Idea of Nature*, trans. M. Chase from *Le voile d'Isis: essai sur l'histoire de l'idée de nature* (Cambridge, Mass.).

Hall, D. L. and Ames, R. T. (1987) *Thinking through Confucius* (New York).

Hamlyn, D. W. (1968) 'Review of Lloyd 1966', *Philosophical Review* 77: 242–5.

Hansen, C. (1983) *Language and Logic in Ancient China* (Ann Arbor).

Harbsmeier, C. (1998) *Science and Civilisation in China*, vol. VII, part 1: *Language and Logic* (Cambridge).

Haugeland, J. (1985) *Artificial Intelligence: The Very Idea* (Cambridge, Mass.)

Helman, D. M. (ed.) (1988) *Analogical Reasoning: Perspectives on Artificial Intelligence, Cognitive Science, and Philosophy* (Dordrecht).

Henare, A., Holbraad, M. and Wastell, S. (eds.) (2007) *Thinking Through Things* (London).

Henrich, J., Heine, S. J. and Norenzayan, A. (2010) 'The weirdest people in the world', *Behavioral and Brain Sciences* 33: 61–83.

Hesse, M. B. (1963) *Models and Analogies in Science* (London).

  (1974) *The Structure of Scientific Inference* (London).

  (1988) 'Theories, family resemblances and analogy', in Helman (1988), 317–40.

Heywood, P. (2012) 'Anthropology and what there is: reflections on "ontology"', *Cambridge Anthropology* 30: 143–51.

Hocart, A. M. (1915) 'Psychology and ethnology', *Folk-Lore* 26: 115–37.

Holbraad, M. (2012) *Truth in Motion* (Chicago).

Holbraad, M. and Pedersen, M. A. (2009) 'Planet M: the intense abstraction of Marilyn Strathern', *Anthropological Theory* 9: 371–94.

Holbraad, M., Pedersen, M. A. and Viveiros de Castro, E. (2014) 'The politics of ontology: anthropological positions', *Cultural Anthropology* Fieldsights 462.

Holyoak, K. J. and Morrison, R. G. (eds.) (2005) *The Cambridge Handbook of Thinking and Reasoning* (Cambridge).

Holyoak, K. J. and Thagard, P. (1989) 'A computational model of analogical problem solving', in Vosniadou and Ortony (1989), 242–66.

  (1995) *Mental Leaps: Analogy in Creative Thought* (Cambridge, Mass.).

Hooper, W. (1794) *Rational Recreations*, 4th rev. edn (London).

Horden, P. and Hsu, E. (eds.) (2013) *The Body in Balance: Humoral Medicine in Practice* (Oxford).

Horton, R. (1967) 'African traditional thought and western science', *Africa* 37: 50–71 and 155–87; abbreviated version in Wilson (1970), 131–71.

Horton, R. and Finnegan, R. (eds.) (1973) *Modes of Thought* (London).

Hsu, E. (2010) 'Qing Hao (Herba Artemisiae Annuae) in the Chinese Materia Medica', in E. Hsu and S. Harris (eds.) *Plants, Health and Healing: On the Interface of Ethnobotany and Medical Anthropology* (Oxford), 83–130.

Hull, D. L. (1976) 'Are species really individuals?', *Systematic Zoology* 25: 174–91.

  (2001) *Science and Selection* (Cambridge).

Humphrey, N. K. (1976) 'The social function of intellect', in P. P. G. Bateson and R. A. Hinde (eds.) *Growing Points in Ethology* (Cambridge), 303–17.

  (1992) *A History of the Mind* (London).

Ingold, T. (2000) *The Perception of the Environment* (London).

Jablonka, E. and Lamb, M. J. (1995) *Epigenetic Inheritance and Evolution* (Oxford).

  (2014) *Evolution in Four Dimensions*, rev. edn (Cambridge, Mass.).

Jackendoff, R. (1996) 'How language helps us think', *Pragmatics and Cognition* 4: 1–34.

Johnston, I. (2010) *The Mozi: A Complete Translation* (Hong Kong).

Kahneman, D. (2011) *Thinking Fast and Slow* (New York).

Kahneman, D., Slovic, P. and Tversky, A. (eds.) (1982) *Judgement under Uncertainty* (Cambridge).

Kedar-Cabelli, S. (1988) 'Analogy – from a unified perspective', in Helman (1988), 65–103.

Keil, F. (1989) *Concepts, Kinds and Cognitive Development* (Cambridge, Mass.).

Keller, E. F. (2000) *The Century of the Gene* (Cambridge, Mass.).

Kepler, J. (1940 [1619]) *Harmonices Mundi*, in *Gesammelte Werke*, vol. vi, ed. M. Caspar (Munich).

   (1968 [1604]) *Ad Vitellionem Paralipomena, quibus astronomiae pars optica traditur* (Frankfurt) (Brussels).

Khalidi, M. A. (2013) *Natural Categories and Human Kinds* (Cambridge).

Knoblock, J. (1988–94) *Xunzi: A Translation and Study of the Complete Works*, 3 vols. (Stanford).

Knoblock, J. and Riegel, J. (2000) *The Annals of Lü Buwei* (Stanford).

Kroeber, A. L. and Kluckhohn, C. (1952) *Culture: A Critical Review of Concepts and Definitions* (Cambridge, Mass.).

Kuhn, T. S. (1970 [1962]) *The Structure of Scientific Revolutions*, 2nd edn (Chicago).

Kuper, A. (1999) *Culture: The Anthropologists' Account* (Cambridge, Mass.).

Laidlaw, J. (2012) 'Ontologically challenged', *Anthropology of this Century* 4 (on-line).

   (2014) *The Subject of Virtue* (Cambridge).

Laidlaw, J. and Heywood, P. (2012) 'One more turn and you're there', *Anthropology of this Century* 5 (on-line).

Lakoff, G. and Johnson, M. (1980) *The Metaphors We Live By* (Chicago).

Larsen, M. T. (1987) 'The Babylonian lukewarm mind: reflections on science, divination and literacy', in Rochberg-Halton (1987), 203–25.

Latour, B. (2013 [2012]) *An Inquiry into Modes of Existence*, trans. C. Porter from *Enquête sur les modes d'existence* (Cambridge, Mass.).

Leavitt, J. (2011) *Linguistic Relativities: Language Diversity and Modern Thought* (Cambridge).

Lenclud, G. (2013) *L'universalisme ou le pari de la raison* (Paris).

Levinson, S. C. (2003) *Space in Language and Cognition* (Cambridge).

Levinson, S. C. and Jaisson, P. (eds.) (2006) *Evolution and Culture* (Cambridge, Mass.).

Lévi-Strauss, C. (1966 [1962]) *The Savage Mind*, trans. from *La pensée sauvage* (London).

Lévy-Bruhl, L. (1926 [1910]) *How Natives Think*, trans. L. A. Clare from *Les fonctions mentales dans les sociétés inférieures* (London).

Lewis, M. E. (2003) 'Custom and human nature in early China', *Philosophy East and West* 53: 308–22.

Livingstone, A. (1986) *Mystical and Mythological Explanatory Works of Assyrian and Babylonian Scholars* (Oxford).

Lloyd, G. E. R. (1966) *Polarity and Analogy* (Cambridge).

   (1973) *Early Greek Science: Thales to Aristotle* (Cambridge).

   (1979) *Magic, Reason and Experience* (Cambridge).

   (1983) *Science, Folklore and Ideology* (Cambridge).

   (1990) *Demystifying Mentalities* (Cambridge).

   (1991) *Methods and Problems in Greek Science* (Cambridge).

(1996a) *Adversaries and Authorities* (Cambridge).

(1996b) *Aristotelian Explorations* (Cambridge).

(2002) *The Ambitions of Curiosity* (Cambridge).

(2003) *In the Grip of Disease* (Oxford).

(2004) *Ancient Worlds, Modern Reflections* (Oxford).

(2007a) *Cognitive Variations* (Oxford).

(2007b) 'The Wife of Philinus, or the doctors' dilemma: medical signs and cases and non-deductive inference', in D. Scott (ed.) *Maieusis* (Oxford), 335–50.

(2009) *Disciplines in the Making* (Oxford).

(2010a) 'The techniques of persuasion and the rhetoric of disorder (luan) in late Zhanguo and Western Han texts', in M. Nylan and M. A. N. Loewe (eds.) *China's Early Empires* (Cambridge), ch. 19, 451–60.

(2010b) 'History and human nature: cross-cultural universals and cultural relativities', *Interdisciplinary Science Reviews* 35: 201–14.

(2012a) *Being, Humanity and Understanding* (Oxford).

(2012b) 'Humanities in a globalized world: vive l'unité, vive la différence', in Zhang Longxi (ed.) *The Concept of Humanity in an Age of Globalization* (Taipei), ch. 14, 217–28.

(2012c) 'The pluralism of Greek "mathematics"', in Chemla (2012), ch. 8, 294–310.

(2013) 'Reasoning and culture in a historical perspective', *Journal of Cognition and Culture* 13: 437–57.

(2014) *The Ideals of Inquiry: An Ancient History* (Oxford).

Lloyd, G. E. R. and Sivin, N. (2002) *The Way and the Word* (New Haven, Conn.).

Long, A. A. and Sedley, D. N. (1987) *The Hellenistic Philosophers*, 2 vols. (Cambridge).

Loraux, N. (2002 [1987]) 'The bond of division', in *The Divided City* (Chicago) ch. 4, 93–122; originally published as 'Le lien de la division', *Le Cahier du Collège international de la philosophie* 4: 101–24.

Lukes, S. (1967) 'Some problems about rationality', *Archives Européennes de Sociologie* 8: 247–64; reprinted in Wilson (1970), 194–213.

Lyons, J. (1995) 'Colour in language', in T. Lamb and J. Bourriau (eds.) *Colour: Art and Science* (Cambridge), ch. 8, 194–224.

MacIntyre, A. (1967) 'The idea of a social science', *Proceedings of the Aristotelian Society Suppl.* 41; reprinted in Wilson (1970), 112–30.

Major, J. S. (1993) *Heaven and Earth in Early Han Thought* (Albany, N.Y.).

Major, J. S. et al. (eds.) (2010) *The Huainanzi* (New York).

Marett, R. R. (1912) 'The study of magico-religious facts', in B. Freire-Marreco and J. L. Myres (eds.) *Notes and Queries on Anthropology*, 4th edn (London), 251–60.

Marriott, M. (1976) 'Hindu transactions: diversity without dualism', in B. Kapferer (ed.) *Transaction and Meaning* (Philadelphia), 109–42.

Mauss, M. (1938) 'Une catégorie de l'esprit humain: la notion de personne, celle de "moi": un plan de travail', *Journal of the Royal Anthropological Institute* 68: 263–81.

Mayr, E. (ed.) (1957) *The Species Problem* (American Association for the Advancement of Science Publications 50) (Washington, D.C.).

Medin, D. and Ortony, A. (1989) 'Psychological essentialism', in Vosniadou and Ortony (1989), 179–95.

Mercier, H. (2011) 'On the universality of argumentative reasoning', *Journal of Cognition and Culture* 11: 85–113.

Mercier, H. and Sperber, D. (2011) 'Why do humans reason? Arguments for an argumentative theory', *Behavioral and Brain Sciences* 34: 57–74.

Métailié, G. (forthcoming) *Science and Civilisation in China*, vol. VI, part 4: *Traditional Botanical Knowledge: An Ethnobotanical Approach* (Cambridge).

Miall, D. S. (ed.) (1982) *Metaphor: Problems and Perspectives* (Brighton).

Mignucci, M. (1981) 'Hōs epi to polu et nécessaire dans la conception aristotélicienne de la science', in E. Berti (ed.) *Aristotle on Science: The Posterior Analytics* (Padua), 173–203.

Mill, J. S. (1875 [1843]) *A System of Logic*, 9th edn (London).

Mosko, M. (2010) 'Partible penitents: dividual personhood and Christian practice in Melanesia and the West', *Journal of the Royal Anthropological Institute NS* 16: 215–40.

Needham, J. (1956) *Science and Civilisation in China*, vol. II: *History of Scientific Thought* (Cambridge).

Needham, R. (1963) 'Introduction' to Durkheim and Mauss (1963), vii–xlviii.

Nersessian, N. J. (2008) *Creating Scientific Concepts* (Cambridge, Mass.).

Nettle, D. (2009) 'Beyond nature versus culture: cultural variation as an evolved characteristic', *Journal of the Royal Anthropological Institute NS* 15: 223–40.

Netz, R. (1999) *The Shaping of Deduction in Greek Mathematics* (Cambridge).

Nickerson, R. S. (1998) 'Confirmation bias: a ubiquitous phenomenon in many guises', *Review of General Psychology* 2: 175–220.

Nisbett, R. E. (2003) *The Geography of Thought: How Asians and Westerners Think Differently and Why* (New York).

Nisbett, R. E. and Ross, L. (1980) *Human Inference: Strategies and Shortcomings of Social Judgement* (Englewood Cliffs, N.J.).

Nylan, M. (2001) *The Five 'Confucian' Classics* (New Haven, Conn.).

Olivelle, P. (1996) *Upaniṣads* (Oxford).

Osborne, C. (2007) *Dumb Beasts and Dead Philosophers* (Oxford).

Paris, J. A. (1843) *Pharmacologia*, 9th edn (London).

Peck, A. L. (1937) *Aristotle, Parts of Animals* (Loeb Classical Library) (London).

Pedersen, M. A. (2011) *Not Quite Shamans: Spirit Worlds and Political Lives in Northern Mongolia* (Ithaca, N.Y.).

(2012) 'Common nonsense: a review of certain recent reviews of the "ontological turn"', *Anthropology of this Century* 5 (on-line).

Perelman, C. and Olbrechts-Tyteca, L. (1969 [1958]) *The New Rhetoric: A Treatise on Argumentation*, trans. J. Wilkinson and P. Weaver from *La nouvelle rhétorique* (Notre Dame, Ind.).

Polya, G. (1954a) *Mathematics and Plausible Reasoning*, vol. I: *Induction and Analogy in Mathematics* (London).

(1954b) *Mathematics and Plausible Reasoning*, vol. II: *Patterns of Plausible Inference* (London).

Prigogine, I. (1980) *From Being to Becoming* (San Francisco).

Prigogine, I. and Stengers, I. (1997) *The End of Certainty: Time, Chaos and the New Laws of Nature* (New York).

Qu Anjing (1997) 'On hypotenuse diagrams in ancient China', *Centaurus* 39: 193–210.

Quine, W. van O. (1960) *Word and Object* (Cambridge, Mass.).

(1969) *Ontological Relativity and Other Essays* (New York).

Randall, J. H. (1961) *The School of Padua and the Emergence of Modern Science* (Padua).

Reding, J.-P. (1985) *Les fondements philosophiques de la rhétorique chez les sophistes grecs et chez les sophistes chinois* (Bern).

Renn, J. (ed.) (2012) *The Globalization of Knowledge in History* (Berlin).

Rivers, W. H. R. (1912) 'The primitive conception of death', *Hibbert Journal* 10: 393–407.

Rochberg, F. (2004) *The Heavenly Writing: Divination, Horoscopy and Astronomy in Mesopotamian Culture* (Cambridge).

Rochberg-Halton, F. (ed.) (1987) *Language, Literature, and History* (American Oriental Society 67) (New Haven, Conn.).

Rorty, R. (1999) *Philosophy and Social Hope* (London).

Ross, N. (2002) 'Cognitive aspects of intergenerational change: mental models, cultural change, and environmental behavior among the Lacandon Maya of Southern Mexico', *Human Organization* 61: 125–38.

Ross, N., Medin, D. L., Coley, J. D. and Atran, S. (2003) 'Cultural and experiential differences in the development of folkbiological induction', *Cognitive Development* 18: 25–47.

Runciman, W. G. (2009) *The Theory of Cultural and Social Selection* (Cambridge).

Ryle, G. (1949) *The Concept of Mind* (London).

Sapir, E. (1949) *Selected Writings of Edward Sapir in Language, Culture, and Personality* (Berkeley).

Schaffer, S. (2010) 'Opposition is true friendship', *Interdisciplinary Science Reviews* 35: 277–90.

Searle, J. R. (1984) *Minds, Brains and Science* (London).

Severi, C. (2013) 'Philosophies without ontology', *HAU: Journal of Ethnographic Theory* 3: 192–6.

Shaughnessy, E. A. (1997) *I Ching: The Classic of Changes* (New York).

Shirokogoroff, S. M. (1935) *Psychomental Complex of the Tungus* (London).

Skorupski, J. (1976) *Symbol and Theory* (Cambridge).

Smith, B. Herrnstein (2011) 'The chimera of relativism', *Common Knowledge* 17: 13–26.

Smolin, L. (2000) *Three Roads to Quantum Gravity* (London).

(2006) *The Trouble with Physics: The Rise of String Theory, the Fall of a Science, and What Comes Next* (London).

Sorabji, R. (1993) *Animal Minds and Human Morals* (London).

Sperber, D. (1975) *Rethinking Symbolism*, trans. A. Morton (Cambridge).

Sperber, D., Premack, D. and Premack, A. J. (eds.) (1995) *Causal Cognition: A Multidisciplinary Debate* (Oxford).

Stengers, I. (2010) *Cosmopolitics*, trans. R. Bononno, 2 vols. (Minneapolis).

(2011) 'Comparison as a matter of concern', *Common Knowledge* 17: 48–63.

Sterckx, R. (2002) *The Animal and the Daemon in Early China* (Albany, N.Y.).

Stich, S. P. (1985) 'Could man be an irrational animal? Some notes on the epistemology of rationality', *Synthèse* 64: 115–35.

Stocking, G. W. (1995) *After Tylor: British Social Anthropology 1888–1951* (Madison).

Strathern, M. (1988) *The Gender of the Gift* (Berkeley).

(1999) *Property, Substance and Effect: Anthropological Essays on Persons and Things* (London).

(2005) *Kinship, Law and the Unexpected* (Cambridge).

Tambiah, S. J. (1968) 'The magical power of words', *Man NS* 3: 175–208.

(1973) 'Form and meaning of magical acts: a point of view', in Horton and Finnegan (1973), 199–229.

(1990) *Magic, Science, Religion and the Scope of Rationality* (Cambridge).

Taylor, A.-C. (2013) 'Distinguishing ontologies', *HAU: Journal of Ethnographic Theory* 3: 201–4.

Thagard, P. (2010) *The Brain and the Meaning of Life* (Princeton, N.J.).

Tooby, J. and Cosmides, L. (1992) 'The psychological foundations of culture', in Barkow, Cosmides and Tooby (1992), 19–136.

Turner, T. S. (2009) 'The crisis of late structuralism. Perspectivism and animism: rethinking culture, nature, spirit, and bodiliness', *Tipiti* 7: 1–42.

Tversky, A. and Kahneman, D. (1974) 'Judgement under uncertainty: heuristics and biases', *Science NS* 185: 1124–31.

Vickers, B. (1984a) 'Analogy versus identity: the rejection of occult symbolism, 1580–1680', in Vickers (1984b), 95–163.

Vickers, B. (ed.) (1984b) *Occult and Scientific Mentalities in the Renaissance* (Cambridge).

Vilaça, A. (2010 [2006]) *Strange Enemies: Indigenous Agency and Scenes of Encounters in Amazonia*, trans. D. Rodgers from *Quem somos nós: os Wari' encontram os brancos* (Durham, N.C.).

(2011) 'Dividuality in Amazonia: God, the devil, and the constitution of personhood in Wari' Christianity', *Journal of the Royal Anthropological Institute, NS* 17: 243–62.

(2013) 'Communicating through difference', *HAU: Journal of Ethnographic Theory* 3: 174–8.

Viveiros de Castro, E. (1998) 'Cosmological deixis and Amerindian perspectivism', *Journal of the Royal Anthropological Institute, NS* 4: 469–88.

(2004) 'Perspectival anthropology and the method of controlled equivocation', *Tipiti* 2.1: 3–22.

(2009) *Métaphysiques cannibales* (Paris).

(2010) 'In some sense', *Interdisciplinary Science Reviews* 35: 318–33.

Vlastos, G. (1991) *Socrates: Ironist and Moral Philosopher* (Cambridge).

Vosniadou, S. and Ortony, A. (1989) *Similarity and Analogical Reasoning* (Cambridge).

Vygotsky, L. (1986) *Thought and Language* (Cambridge, Mass.).

Wagner, R. (1975) *The Invention of Culture* (Englewood Cliffs, N.J.).

(1991) 'The fractal person', in M. Godelier and M. Strathern (eds.) *Big Men and Great Men* (Cambridge), 159–73.

Wardy, R. B. B. (2000) *Aristotle in China: Language, Categories and Translation* (Cambridge).

(2005) 'The mysterious Aristotelian olive', *Science in Context* 18: 69–91.

Watson, R. and Horowitz, W. (2011) *Writing Science Before the Greeks* (Leiden).

Whitehead, A. N. (1978 [1929]) *Process and Reality*, corrected edn, ed. D. R. Griffin and D. W. Sherburne (New York).

Whorf, B. L. (1967 [1956]) *Language, Thought and Reality*, ed. J. Carroll (Cambridge, Mass.).

Wilson, B. R. (ed.) (1970) *Rationality* (Oxford).

Winch, P. (1958) *The Idea of a Social Science* (London).

(1964) 'Understanding a primitive society', *American Philosophical Quarterly* 1: 307–24; reprinted in Wilson (1970), 78–111.

Wittgenstein, L. (1953) *Philosophical Investigations*, trans. G. E. M. Anscombe (Oxford).

Index

Achuar, 19, 27
actors' versus observers' categories, 15, 22, 27, 38, 47
agency, 16, 18, 27, 38, 104, 110
Amazonia, 19, 30
ambiguity, 1, 5, 24–5, 114
analogism, 8, 17, 79, 84, 100–2
anarchy, 44
Anaxagoras, 73–5
animals, 15, 17, 22–3, 30, 32, 34, 38–40, 47, 51, 60–1, 78, 80–7, 90–6, 99, 110–11, 113, 120
appearance/reality, 23, 89
Araweté, 19, 21, 27
Archimedes, 59, 68–9
Aristarchus, 118
Aristotle, 5, 7, 15, 25, 39, 49–51, 53–7, 58, 60–1, 68, 72, 74, 83, 86–7, 94–7, 99, 103, 105–6, 109–14, 117, 119–20
  on analogy, 79–83
  on demonstration, 50, 79–82, 111
assemblies, 68, 111
astronomy, 15, 54
Atran, S., 88, 91–3, 96
Augustine, 93
Austin, J. L., 74
axiomatics, 51, 53, 55, 62, 65, 69–70, 110–11
Azande, 75

blood, 18, 78, 81–2, 101, 105
bodies, 8, 17, 19, 21, 32–3, 45, 73, 84, 95–6, 101–2, 105

Carroll, Lewis, 65
causation, 16, 18, 21, 27, 38, 74–5, 77–9, 87, 97, 104–5, 110
Cavalieri, B., 69–70
certainty, 5, 9, 68, 119
Chang, Hasok, 112
charity in interpretation, 15
chemistry, 90, 112–13, 118

Christianity, 15, 33, 119
Chunyu Yi, 77
classification, 8, 81, 88–9, 91, 93, 111
coinage of terms, 5, 15, 82
colour, 24–5, 76, 95, 108, 110, 115
common sense, 57, 92, 96, 103, 117
comparatism, 6, 29–42
computers, 58–9, 110, 120
conceptual frameworks, 6, 26, 29, 104, 106, 114
Confucius, 44n1, 46
conjecture, 1, 71–3, 79, 82–3
consistency, 56
Copernicus, 15
correlations, 77–9, 83–4, 98
correspondence, 17, 60, 75–7, 82, 84
cosmologies, 3–4, 9, 20, 27, 29, 38, 44–5, 71, 90, 97–9, 104, 106
counter-intuitiveness, 10, 15–16, 104, 116
courage, 50, 113–14
culture, 8–10, 17, 20, 22–3, 39–40, 101, 110, 116

Daodejing, 12–14
Darwin, C., 92, 118
Davidson, D., 15
deception, 5, 8, 13–14, 49, 52–4, 58, 79, 115, 120
definition, 1, 15, 24, 40, 49, 51, 56, 60, 62, 79–80, 82, 87, 109–11, 114
democracy, 44, 117
Democritus, 72, 97
demonstration, 4–5, 50, 53, 59–63, 68–71, 79–80, 82, 110, 117
Descola, P., 8, 10, 16, 17–18, 20, 37–8, 79, 84, 100–2, 105–6, 115
diagrams, 59, 63–7
dichotomies, 9–10, 12, 20, 23, 27, 40, 110, 116
disease, 1, 21, 45, 50, 74–5, 90, 92–4, 118
Dorze, 15–16

ecology, 17, 85, 91
Egypt, 21, 32
Einstein, A., 15
Empedocles, 49
Epicureans, 97
epistemology, 25–6, 71, 100
equivocation, 18, 87
error, 7, 16, 27, 37, 52–4, 87, 113, 116, 118
Erya, 85
essentialism, 90, 93–4, 113
ethics, 4, 6, 29, 35, 40, 43–57, 113
ethology, 7, 39, 84
Euclid, 51, 59, 62–3, 65, 68
Evans-Pritchard, E. E., 15–16, 75
evolution, 39, 84, 92, 105, 118
experiment, 7, 106, 110
explanation, 1, 4, 21, 53, 75, 78, 82, 99

faith, 36
felicity, 74, 77–9, 118
Feyerabend, P., 24
fire, 86, 95–8
five phases, 60, 76–8, 83–5, 97–8
Fludd, R., 60, 71–2
Frazer, J. G., 74

Galen, 53
Galileo, 15
genera/species, 3, 5, 23, 87–8, 92, 94
general terms, 2–3, 41, 57, 60, 83, 87–8
Genesis, 30, 39
gods, 21, 32–3, 35–6, 38, 118
Gongsun Long, 107
Grand Unified Theory, 36

Hanfeizi, 56n14
harmony, 45–6, 71, 77
health, 1, 45, 118
Heisenberg, W., 105
Heraclitus, 46, 96
Herodotus, 32, 34, 73
Hesse, M., 58
heuristics, 6, 58–87
Hippocratic writings, 32n2, 73, 78, 111
Hong Fan, 98
Huainanzi, 26n19, 75n22, 77, 83, 85, 99, 108
Hui Shi, 52, 78
humans, 17–19, 22, 30, 33–4, 38–41, 44, 47–8, 56, 73, 83–6, 91, 96, 101–2, 104, 110, 116
hypotheses, 83, 106

incommensurability, 14–15
inconclusiveness, 6, 54

incontrovertibility, 51, 53, 62, 68, 111
indeterminacy, 2, 14
India, 37n8, 64
induction, 54, 58
ineffability, 36
inexpressibility, 2, 12, 14
inscrutability, 2, 14
intelligibility, 4–6, 10–28, 31, 35, 37, 100, 102
interiority, 17, 27, 84, 101–2, 105, 115
Itza Maya, 88, 91

Jesuits, 33, 51, 62
Jiuzhang suanshu, see Nine Chapters on Mathematical Procedures
jurisprudence, 56

Kant, I., 41, 116
Kepler, J., 58, 60, 69–72, 120
Kuhn, T., 14–15

language, 2–4, 13, 19, 26, 33, 40, 88, 97, 107–8, 121
   natural, 2–3, 5–6, 10–11, 13, 25, 29, 38, 41, 60, 74, 84, 87, 88–9, 97
Law of Excluded Middle, 106
Law of Non-Contradiction, 106
law-courts, 68, 111
Liezi, 85, 85n32
literacy, 21, 35
literal, 5–6, 9, 12–13, 15, 43, 110, 114
Liu Hui, 59, 61–2
Lunyu, 44n1, 46n4
Lüshi chunqiu, 34–5, 45, 51–3, 78–9, 112

malaria, 118
male/female, 34, 46
marriage, 32, 39
mathematics, 50–1, 53, 59, 61–72, 110–11
measurement, 1, 71, 106, 110
Mencius, 47–8, 56, 114
metamorphosis, 85
metaphor, 5–6, 9, 12–13, 15, 43, 49–50, 60, 79, 106, 110, 114
microcosm–macrocosm, 44, 71
modus ponens, 56
modus tollens, 55–6
Mohists, 15n5
monarchy, 44
monotheism, 32–3, 119
Mozi, 116n4
multidimensionality, 5, 9–10, 23–4, 26–7, 40, 87, 90, 100, 106, 110, 115–16
music, 13, 45–6, 71
mysteries, 72, 76
mystification, 11, 33, 37

nature, 2–3, 8–10, 16–17, 20–3, 27, 39–40, 58, 72, 86, 94, 101, 110, 116
Netz, R., 63
Newton, I., 15
Nine Chapters on Mathematical Procedures, 51n9, 61–2, 64
Nuer, 15–16

oligarchy, 44
omens, 21
ontologies, 4, 8, 10, 16–18, 20, 23, 25, 27, 37–40, 61, 88–107, 115
Orientalism, 32

paradigms, 14–15, 54, 83, 96, 113
paradox, 37, 52, 65, 107
parallelism, 54, 76
Parmenides, 18, 103, 116
Persia, 32
person, 16, 19, 27, 38, 84, 102, 104, 110
perspectivism, 10, 16, 18–20, 101–2
persuasion, 5, 51, 53, 67–8, 110–11
phronēsis, 51, 55, 57
physicality, 8, 17, 27, 84, 101–2, 115
Pindar, 112
planets, 71–2, 90
plants, 23, 60, 82–4, 86–7, 90, 93–4, 99
Plato, 2, 5, 46, 48–9, 50, 52–3, 66–8, 71–2, 86, 102, 107, 109–11, 114, 116–17, 120
    Forms, 49, 66–7, 95
Pleistocene, 93
pluralism, 5, 21, 26, 40, 61, 90, 115, 119
poetry, 49–51
politics, 31, 35, 39, 44–7, 50, 52–3, 68, 79, 84, 97, 99, 111, 117, 119
polytheism, 32–3
predators/prey, 17–18, 92–3, 101
processes, 94–7, 99–100, 105
Proclus, 53, 72
progress, 1, 37, 40, 90, 110
proportion, 61, 70–2
prosperity, 2, 119
psychiatry, 105
Ptolemy, 15, 71
Pyrrhonists, 97
Pythagoreans, 46, 74

Qin Shi Huang Di, 45–6
Quine, W. van O., 2, 14–15

realism, 5, 9–10, 23, 27, 110, 115
reality, 3, 5, 8, 10, 23–4, 27, 36, 89, 90, 97–8, 100, 102–4, 115–16

reductio, 55, 59, 68
reductionism, 6, 13, 26
reference, 2, 14, 25, 112
regularity, 21–2, 116
relativism, 2–3, 5, 9, 10, 23–4, 27, 90, 110, 115
religion, 11, 22, 29, 31–3, 35–6, 38, 84, 94, 117, 119
replicability, 1, 110
revisability, 6, 16, 26–7, 40–2, 102, 104, 106–7, 109–10, 114, 120
rhetoric, 49–51
Ricci, M., 33
ritual, 13, 19, 33, 36, 74–5, 79, 118
rivalry, 21, 109, 111–12

sages, 12, 35, 45, 52–5, 57
scepticism, 35, 78, 90, 97, 103
self-evidence, 50–1, 53, 55, 111
semantic stretch, 5–6, 9, 12–13, 26–7, 40, 87, 106–7, 110, 114, 118, 120
sense/reference, 15, 19, 112
Severi, C., 18, 27
shamans, 19, 31, 101–2
Shanhaijing, 34
Shiji, 46n5, 77
Shuoyuan, 52
signatures, 7, 74
slaves, 46
Socrates, 48–9, 52, 102, 113–14, 117
space, 18, 27, 38, 91, 104, 104n25, 110
Stengers, I., 31
Stoics, 35n5, 55, 97
style, 49–50, 110
subjectivity, 2
substance, 18–19, 74, 94–6, 98–101, 105, 112–13
syllogism, 50, 54–5, 79
symbols, 21, 60, 71, 74, 77, 119
systematicity, 18

Tambiah, S. J., 74
technology, 2
Terence, 121
Thales, 112
theology, 16, 36, 51, 53
Theophrastus, 72, 82–3, 86, 96–7
time, 18, 27, 91, 93, 108
translation, 2, 6, 10–12, 16, 18–20, 24, 27–8, 90, 100, 109
tyrants, 32, 35

universals, cross-cultural, 4, 23–4, 84
univocity, 1, 5, 26, 40, 50, 79, 87, 109–10, 114, 117

validity, 29, 41, 58, 79, 90, 110
verification, 1, 73, 80, 82
Viveiros de Castro, E., 8, 10, 16–21, 23, 100–2, 106, 116
voting, 53, 111

water, 47, 86, 96–8, 112–13
welfare, 1, 109, 117, 119
Wittgenstein, L., 12–13

Xenophanes, 32
Xunzi, 47–8, 85–6

Yijing (*Book of Changes*), 76

Zeus, 21
Zhoubi suanjing, 62
Zhouli, 85
Zhuangzi, 12n3, 26, 78, 85, 98, 116